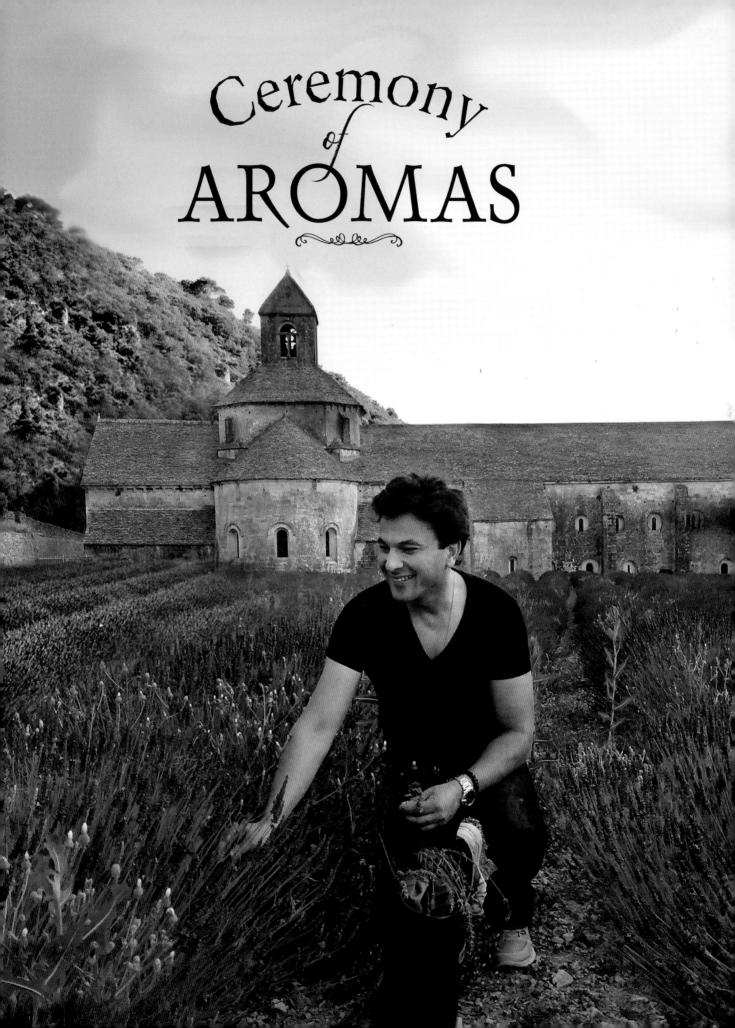

Ceremony
of
AROMAS

BLOOMSBURY INDIA
Bloomsbury Publishing India Pvt. Ltd
Second Floor, LSC Building No. 4, DDA Complex, Pocket C – 6 & 7,
Vasant Kunj, New Delhi 110070

BLOOMSBURY, BLOOMSBURY INDIA and the Diana logo are
trademarks of Bloomsbury Publishing Plc

First published in India 2023
This edition published 2023

ISBN: 978-93-56408-73-9
2 4 6 8 10 9 7 5 3 1

Printed and bound in India by Thomson Press India Ltd

To find out more about our authors and books, visit
www.bloomsbury.com and sign up for our newsletters

Ceremony
of
AROMAS

Spices ⦁ Flavours ⦁ Recipes & More

VIKAS KHANNA

BLOOMSBURY
NEW DELHI ⦁ LONDON ⦁ OXFORD ⦁ NEW YORK ⦁ SYDNEY

Contents

Warm Carrot and Cranberry Medley in
    Sage-Cardamom Butter
Coconut Simmered Pan-Roasted Chicken
Ricotta-Stuffed Baked Cauliflower
Soba Noodles with Star Anise-Infused Oil
Homemade Gingerade
Satiny Ginger Chocolate Ice Cream

Kokum ... 169

Coconut and Kokum Welcome Drink
Green Mango and Lamb Salad
Dried Shrimp Stir-Fry with Kokum
Mrs Pacheco's Fish Curry
Pan-Fried Crispy Eggplant
Bartlett Pear and Corn Pulao
Kokum Sandalwood Cooler

Lavender ... 187

Gailon Broccoli and Labneh Soup
Purple Asparagus with Lavender Salt
Chioggia Beet with Passion Fruit and
    Lavender Vinaigrette
Lavender Butter-Tossed Romanesco
    with Blood Orange Segments
Lavender Honey Roast Chicken
Red Quinoa with Orange Habanero
Blackberry and Lavender Jam Tarts
Lavender and Pineberry Cooler

Mango Powder ... 207

Noodle and Vegetable Broth with Yuzu
Crabmeat Croquette Salad
Family Favourite Peach Frittata
Green Mango and Shrimp Curry
Crispy Okra with Mango Powder Spice Mix
Vetiver and Green Mango Shrub
Strawberry and Vanilla Cream with Meringue

Mustard ... 225

Coconut Chicken Soup with Mustard
Mustard Dips
Grilled Chicken in Smoky Mustard Oil

Steamed Apple Butter Herring
Ginger-Scented Creamy Mustard Greens
Tamarind Mustard Rice
Fermented Carrot and Mustard Drink
White Chocolate and French Mustard Cake

Nutmeg and Mace ... 245

Spinach, Corn and Shrimp Soup
Purple Yam and Potato Rosti
Comforting Chicken Tarts
Creamy Parmesan Cheese Noodles
Mace and Black Pepper Apple Cider

Pippali ... 259

Creamy Almond Mushroom Soup
Boston Lettuce with Pippali Dressing
Soy Granules Shepherd's Pie
Spiced Tomato Rice with Poached Eggs
Black Chickpeas and Green Mango Pilaf
Strawberry Rhubarb Medley
Mint-Pippali Coffee Pudding

Saffron ... 277

Coconut Saffron Clam Soup
Summer Watermelon Salad
Apple Cider Roast Chicken
Smoky Mashed Potatoes
Almond Milk Rice Pilaf
Honey, Tangerine and Saffron Marmalade
Sparkling Saffron Apple Fizz
Ginger Saffron Yogurt Cake

Star Anise ... 297

Chinese Five-Spice Vegetable Soup
Summertime Lamb and Rice Salad
Creamy Puy Lentils with Lamb Shanks
Asian Tofu and Spaghetti
Tea-Infused Vegetable Pulao
Apple, Cranberry and Star Anise Chutney
Ginger-Star Anise Apple Juice
Chickpeas and Apricot Rice Pudding

I Slept Last Night in a Little Spice Farm

I slept last night in a little spice farm
Nature has awoken me, not an alarm
Hearing musical sounds of the birds
Silent modesty in their lyrical words
Chanting to wet soil below my feet
Bright blossoms woven into wreaths
Fresh dews resting every leaf
Creating nature's sacred motif works
All night through, without any perks
The powerful lean vines of peppers
Clinging and saying, we are together
Their tiny claws holding on to the tree
Nutmeg fruit just opened, saying I'm free
Cardamom flowers sang to the earth
Tamarind pods are soon given birth
Liquorice cologne of the fennel seeds
Sprawling sun-like mustard field proceed
Turmeric said, don't forget me please
I can bring pilgrims to their knees
I'm nipped right in the bud, says a clove
Created in clusters, I am a treasure trove
Saffron elevates life through every strand
When plucked by the gentlest hand
New lands found, routes discovered
Many wars fought, slowly recovered
Disappearance and reappearance
They exemplify pure perseverance
Seeds are the sonnets of the gods
To their power the world applauds
Not letting a moment freeze in time
But to live it forever as a wind chime
Inside every spice hides a cosmos
I can smell and feel them so close
Mesmerised by their magical charm
I slept last night in a little spice farm

Introduction

I could hear my heart pumping as beads of sweat dotted my forehead on a hot summer day in Amritsar. I was about to commit yet another sin. Yes, stealing is a sin and I had been told that a million times.

Every time I got caught, I would get the same lecture, 'Look at your brother and sister. You never see them stealing this stuff. And the bigger crime is stealing at home.' I would look back and pretend to be angry while saying, 'Even Lord Krishna used to steal at home.'

This particular conversation would not end like political debates on TV. The truth is I didn't care for any scolding, as it was all a small crust on a large pie of love. Moreover, after finishing my tasting, nothing bothered me, I did not even care to defend myself.

The little spice room behind the kitchen—damp walls, large aluminium containers, pickle jars, sacks of rice and wheat and so much more—was like a treasure trove. The only place where I wanted to be. The only place that made me come to life. I had just stolen a heritage lemon pickle. The age of which was so versatile as if it never had a concept of time. Some days it was 200 years old (the house was 125 years old, so was it before the house was made). One of the keepers of the pickle would say, 'Almost 125-year-old pickle, as old as the house.'

There were debates on the age of this pickle at the table as if it was a national security issue. I was amazed by the crystallised pieces of lemon, which had turned black, and the crystals of salt (lots of salt) and the cumin-carom seeds. Neither locks nor scolding could keep me away from these spice jars.

Well, I was also given the nickname 'masala chor', the thief of spices.

I must confess that I had the most rewarding childhood. Someday I wanted to be a chef and someday just a farmer. I would think that nature is so simple that I can just hide a few seeds of cumin or cardamom, and they will turn into trees. Well, it does not work like that though I did try a lot of times to make it happen.

It was only mustard that I could grow in the northern state of Punjab where I grew up. In the 1990s, the mustard field became the symbol of love for me.

An epic Bollywood movie, a love story—*Dilwale Dulhaniya Le Jayenge*—was released in 1995 and the heart of the nation was lost to these golden fields of sunshine. We all sighed when Punjab was shown as a large carpet of yellow flowers, glistening in the winter sun where the young lovers—Raj and Simran—were united. So, our entire generation went wandering in these fields looking for our Simrans.

A significant part of our lives revolved around these farms and we wondered how this bright and glorious colour was selected for this blossom. I followed the entire step-by-step process of the birth of the mustard seed, watching with fascination the insanely beautiful journey, the blossoming, the metamorphosis and the immortality of Nature... how it keeps itself alive.

I was not a very bright student in school. I always wondered why in India, to succeed in education, you needed to memorise every word in the textbook and reproduce it exactly in the same way. My elder brother Nishant was the best student teachers could ask for. I was the opposite, but like many younger siblings, I took up the same subjects as him (engineering). I thought that medicine was hard, so this must be just the opposite. I had no clue that I was sinking neck-deep into a whole lot of physics and chemistry.

I understood nothing. I was always a backbencher, always behind everyone else and every time a teacher would threaten me for doing badly, I would instantly go to his or her house and request private tuition. At one point, I had knocked on the door of every teacher in the hope that they would help me pass my exams.

I remember sitting in my physics private tuition class as the finals were drawing near. Winter was in full bloom, as were the mustard fields. On my way to tuition, I had plucked a few stems of the plant. When my professor asked me to define infinity, I forgot what I had memorised.

My eyes were moist, I knew I didn't know the answer to his question, and nobody wanted to hear anything other than a perfectly memorised answer. I just showed him the mustard and explained the life cycle of the plant. I knew so much about the times, the dates and the stages that I went on talking on the subject this is the first time, I had a lot to say. When I popped opened a pod and the seeds fell off, I told him, 'This is not the end, it's just the beginning for the next crop. Its power is infinite. When given the right amount of sun, water, temperature… it would blossom again. But if we bury it in wrong conditions, it will forever be lost.'

Everyone was silent. My professor said, 'This theory does not apply here, hope you will find the right question someday for this answer.'

I never passed his class, but I did find the right question for it.

What is the power of a seed?
Infinite

I had already become a food hermit at a young age. Nothing got me more interested in waking up in the morning than a cooking session or training in the kitchen. I even went to Nepal in 1992 to work at Soaltee Oberoi (now known as Crowne Plaza, Kathmandu-Soaltee) and more than the training, it was a classmate's family who made my trip worthwhile. They had black cardamom farms. The first time he mentioned that the black cardamom flowers were blooming, I asked in disbelief, 'Black cardamom has flowers? Since when?'

He told me that even though the spice isn't really pretty, the flowers are divinely pink. This was another metamorphosis that reaches infinity.

Very slowly, over the next few decades, I dedicated all my energy and my life to these little gifts of nature. Every time I would find the genesis of a spice and lay them on a table to photograph, it felt like heaven. Many times, there was a struggle to discover all the stages of the life of a spice. But we did not stop exploring the possibilities.

It felt like the greatest challenge, like bringing the whole family together. It was like the moment when a talent wins an Academy Award and they thank their family and, just for a moment, the faces of the parents are shown. Their roots and origins are recognised and applauded.

Maybe the buds, flowers, stages of maturing don't last forever, but for a moment, they were present in the same period of time and we photographed it. It was a great challenge, a continuous juggling of my travels between India and the US, and the counting of days and seasons and phone calls across different times zones—and it was fun.

Once, I was having a conversation with an astronaut from NASA about traces of water being found on Mars. And all I could talk about was the way black pepper pollinates. I got carried away and kept telling him about how drops of water are the pollen carriers, how the umbrella-like leaves are a shield from the heavy winds, and about the precision of nature and time. I was a little embarrassed later, but not at all apologetic for my love for the process.

One of the greatest revelations of my existence was in the magical realm of saffron fields in the Himalayan valleys of Kashmir. Nature not only creates, she also protects. As it began to drizzle and then rain came pouring down, the petals of saffron blossoms came together and closed, sealing the treasures within. As I stood there waiting, I captured a bee stealing pollen at the exact moment the petals opened as the rain stopped.

Jean Gino truly said, 'Lavender is the soul of Provence.'

As I sat in the lavender fields of the Abbey Notre-Dame de Sénanque, even the sun seemed not to want to leave the scent and beauty of these glorious fields, and so daylight stretched beyond the usual time for sunset.

That moment was only between me and nature,
and the rest of the world had disappeared.

For me, this book is a combination of horticulture, cooking, travelling and an opportunity to live my life as a spice farmer (what a title that would be!) and to live it every day. Many times, I cancelled my tickets and stayed an extra day to understand the spices and how they grow. I still remember the heavy rains in Hoi No just when, at the Vietnam Star Anise Processing and Exporting Company, star anise had been spread out on the concrete floor to dry out. The workers took it in their stride and my guide Huyen Lisa said they considered rains to be a blessing of nature, in spite of the inopportune time of their arrival.

Later, I travelled with the team to the jungles of Vietnam to observe the stages of life of the star anise.

On my way back to the US, I was writing notes as to how the metamorphosis of the butterfly is similar to that of the star anise. A simple sweet-sour, star-shaped fruit goes through extreme temperatures and lengths of drying and finally opening up its wings to form a perfect star anise.

Or it could be pollinating vanilla flowers! Nature is self dependent, it doesn't rely on humans, while humans rely on her completely and gratefully. Vanilla is an exception; humans, fingertips, vision and soft touch is why vanilla is born. Though this globally favourite ice-cream flavour goes through a series of patient processing, but pollinating is something magical. Early in the morning, when the delicate orchid blossoms, lasting only for about 24 hours, the pollen is gently removed with a toothpick and placed behind the rostellum cap. If all goes well, within a few months, this will become a vanilla pod.

But this ethos of delicate growth, step by step, which I call the silent prayers of nature, is common to all living miracles. To witness this at every stage, from genesis in farms to kitchens, adding the spice to the dish and bringing it back to life through flavours—is a true celebration of the journey of blossoms.

Black Pepper

Black Pepper

Black pepper (*Piper nigrum*) is a perennial, evergreen vine, native to the southern region of India. The word pepper is derived from pipor—Old English.

A tropical plant, pepper grows well in hot climatic conditions with high humidity and rainfall. As the vine grows, it attaches itself to trees or needs support in the form of treated poles. The leaves of this plant are pointed and oblong, while small white flowers form oblong spikes and then clusters. The peppercorns are formed in chains, green, which turn to red as they ripen.

The berries are ripe for picking when they turn red, about nine months from flowering. Over a couple of months, they ripen—from green, they turn yellow and then red, and are picked weekly or fortnightly. The harvesting period is from November to March.

At present, Vietnam is the largest cultivator and exporter of this prized spice, which is in demand worldwide in its varied forms.

The unripe green fruit of the plant is dried after being cooked and cleaned in hot water. The thin walls of the fleshy drupes burst in hot water and this, in turn, helps with the browning process when the fruit is dried in the sun or by a machine. The process results in black peppercorn with a thin, wrinkled skin surrounding the seed of the fruit.

Black pepper is obtained by grinding the peppercorns, which also yield pepper oil and pepper spirit.

For white pepper, the berries are picked when the fruit is ripe red and the flesh is removed via fermentation. The seeds are then washed to reveal the clean grey-broken peppercorn. The preferred colour is creamy white.

Green pepper is unripe fruit, treated to retain green colour via chemicals and processes like freeze-drying, while orange or red peppercorns are ripe red fruits. Pink peppercorns belong to another pepper family—the Peruvian pepper tree.

With the distinction of being the most-traded spice in the world, black pepper is sought after as a spice and seasoning along with salt, and is also valued for its medicinal properties to cure a multitude of ailments.

The spiciness of the black pepper comes from piperine. The dried outer layer imparts a woody note filled with floral, citrusy tones, which is not present in white pepper.

To retain the spicy flavour and aroma of pepper, store in airtight containers away from light. Grinding leads to faster flavour evaporation, so it should be ground fresh for best results.

Apple and Coconut Soup

Comforting Sweet Potato and
Parmesan Salad

Zucchini and Arugula Salad with
Ginger Dressing

Green Peppercorns and Honey Prawns

Orange Blossom Rice Cakes

Peppery Spinach and Rice Porridge

Almond Milk and Black Pepper Cooler

Pineapple and White Pepper Granita

Apple and Coconut Soup

The sourness of a Granny Smith apple combined with the fragrance of curry leaves is a very soothing and comforting combination. Coconut milk adds a nice silkiness to the soup. Sometimes, I serve lemon wedges on the side, which help balance the heat from the black pepper.

Serves 4 to 6

Ingredients

2 tablespoons coconut or vegetable oil

1 medium red onion, finely chopped

1 teaspoon mustard seeds

6 to 8 curry leaves

4 teaspoons curry powder

2 to 3 dried red chillies

4 cups chicken or vegetable stock

1 Granny Smith apple, peeled, cored, diced and pureed

1 cup basmati rice, cooked

½ cup coconut milk

Salt to taste

1 tablespoon finely ground black pepper

Directions

Heat oil in a large stockpot over medium heat. Add onion, mustard seeds and curry leaves, and cook, stirring, until the onion is translucent, about 2 to 3 minutes.

Add curry powder, red chillies, stock, apple puree and rice, and bring to a boil. Reduce heat to low and simmer, covered, for 10 to 15 minutes, until the flavours are well combined.

Stir in the coconut milk, salt and pepper. Cook for another 3 to 4 minutes or till desired consistency.

Ladle the soup into bowls and serve hot.

Comforting Sweet Potato and Parmesan Salad

Sweet potatoes are baked along with yellow and red peppers in this simple but vibrant salad that's tossed in a rich savoury dressing of olive oil, garlic and Parmesan.

Serves 4

Ingredients

1 tablespoon minced garlic

1/8 cup Parmesan shavings, plus more for garnish

1/4 cup olive oil

1 teaspoon salt, or to taste

1 teaspoon black pepper

1 cup sweet potato, cut into batons

1 medium-size yellow pepper, deseeded and coarsely chopped

1 medium-size red pepper, deseeded and coarsely chopped

2 tablespoons olive oil

Salt to taste

1 teaspoon black pepper

2 cups romaine lettuce, coarsely torn

Directions

To make the dressing, whisk together garlic, Parmesan, olive oil, salt and black pepper in a small mixing bowl, and refrigerate.

Preheat the oven to 375°F.

In a mixing bowl, toss the sweet potato, yellow and red peppers in olive oil, salt and black pepper.

Line a baking sheet with aluminium foil and place the potato and pepper mixture on it in a single layer. Bake until the vegetables are lightly charred and cooked through, about 10 to 15 minutes.

Remove from oven and let cool to room temperature.

In a salad bowl, combine baked vegetables and romaine lettuce. Drizzle with the Parmesan dressing, garnish with Parmesan shavings and serve.

Zucchini and Arugula Salad with Ginger Dressing

Crunchy zucchini infused with ginger and lemon is a refreshing, quick and light recipe for me. It takes just a few minutes to put together. You can also add heirloom tomatoes for colour, texture and sourness. I like to make the dressing in large batches to use in various recipes; it lasts in the refrigerator for up to a week.

Serves 4

Ingredients

Juice of 1 lemon

1 tablespoon fresh ginger juice

2 tablespoons extra-virgin olive oil

1 teaspoon salt, or to taste

1 teaspoon black pepper

1 medium green zucchini, thinly sliced

1 medium yellow zucchini, thinly sliced

1 cup arugula

2 tablespoons shaved Parmesan cheese

Coarsely ground black pepper for garnish

Directions

In a small mixing bowl, whisk together lemon and ginger juices, oil, salt and black pepper. Add zucchini slices and toss in the dressing until well coated. Let it rest for 5 to 10 minutes at room temperature.

Add arugula, garnish with shaved Parmesan cheese and black pepper, and serve.

Green Peppercorns and Honey Prawns

The balanced sweetness of honey and the aroma of green peppercorns is always a magical combination that works well with any main ingredient, whether it is tofu, mixed vegetables or prawns, as in this case. At times, I prefer to use smaller prawns as they have more flavour.

Serves 4

Ingredients

2 tablespoons sesame oil

3 cloves garlic, finely chopped

1 tablespoon honey

1 tablespoon hot sauce

1 tablespoon rice vinegar

2 tablespoons green peppercorns

Salt to taste

24 medium prawns, deveined

1 medium red onion, thinly sliced

1 teaspoon white pepper

Chives for garnish

Directions

Heat oil in a wok over high heat. Sauté garlic until fragrant. Add honey, hot sauce, rice vinegar, green peppercorns and salt, and cook for about a minute, until the flavours are well combined.

Toss in the prawns, onion and white pepper, and mix to coat well. Cook for about 2 to 3 minutes, until the prawns are cooked through.

Garnish with chives and serve hot.

Orange Blossom Rice Cakes

Crispy rice cakes add the perfect bite to this vegetable medley of mushroom, spinach and baby corn. The flavour of orange blossoms adds a wonderful floral note to the pan-fried rice cakes. Sometimes I also add herbs for a new taste dimension.

Serves 4 to 6

Ingredients

1 cup short-grain rice, rinsed and drained

1 cup coconut milk

1 cup chicken or vegetable stock

2 cloves garlic, chopped

Salt to taste

2 tablespoons rice vinegar

1 tablespoon mirin

Few drops of orange blossom water

1 teaspoon sugar

2 tablespoons canola oil, or as required

1 tablespoon sesame oil

1-inch ginger, peeled and minced

1 cup spinach

10 to 12 baby corn, cut into half

6 to 8 cherry tomatoes, cut into half

6 to 8 button mushrooms, coarsely sliced

1 teaspoon soy sauce

Salt to taste

1 teaspoon coarsely ground black pepper, or to taste

Directions

To make the rice cakes, combine the rice, coconut milk, stock, garlic and salt in a medium saucepan over high heat and bring to a boil. Reduce heat to low and simmer, covered, until the rice is cooked, about 8 to 10 minutes.

Remove from heat and transfer to a wooden bowl. Stir in rice vinegar, mirin, orange blossom water and sugar. Divide into equal lemon-size patties.

Heat oil in a non-stick saucepan over medium-high heat. Add the rice cakes and fry until golden brown, about 1 to 2 minutes each side. Remove with a slotted spoon and drain on a paper towel.

Heat the sesame oil in a wok over high heat. Add ginger and cook for a minute. Add spinach, baby corn, cherry tomatoes, mushrooms, soy sauce, salt and black pepper. Toss together until the vegetables are well-seasoned.

Transfer to a serving dish, top with rice cakes and serve.

Peppery Spinach and Rice Porridge

This is a variation of the all-time favourite Indian comfort food khichdi, a basic lentil and rice dish. Fresh turmeric has been valued for its medicinal properties for centuries and offers a healthy kick along with spinach to make this into a hearty complete meal.

Serves 4

Ingredients

1 cup short-grain rice,
soaked for 1 hour and drained

½ cup split black lentils,
soaked for 1 hour and drained

1-inch piece of fresh turmeric, peeled and minced

1 tablespoon clarified or regular butter

Salt to taste

3 cups spinach, blanched and pureed

½ cup tomatoes, chopped

1 teaspoon green peppercorns, freshly crushed

Directions

Combine the rice, lentils, fresh turmeric, clarified butter, salt and about 4½ cups of water in a large saucepan over high heat and bring to a boil. Reduce heat to low and simmer, covered, until the rice and lentils are cooked, about 20 minutes.

Add spinach puree and tomatoes and ½ teaspoon of green peppercorns and cook to a thick and porridge-like consistency. Add more salt if required.

Garnish with the remaining green peppercorns and serve hot.

Almond Milk and Black Pepper Cooler

A cooling festive drink, this recipe is rich with the goodness and flavours of almonds, cashews and cardamom. Black peppercorns add heat and a contrasting flavour profile to the sweet and creamy almond milk.

Serves 4

Ingredients

1 cup almonds, soaked overnight and drained

2 tablespoons cashew nuts

2 tablespoons lightly roasted hazelnuts

2 cups whole milk

4 tablespoons honey, or to taste

Pinch of cardamom powder

½ teaspoon rose essence

Few strands of saffron

Mint leaves for garnish

1 teaspoon black peppercorns, coarsely crushed

Directions

Combine the almonds, cashews, hazelnuts and milk to process into a smooth puree. Strain into a pitcher using cheesecloth or a fine mesh strainer.

Add honey, cardamom powder and rose essence, and mix well. Add enough water to achieve desired consistency. Cover and refrigerate for at least 2 hours.

Serve over ice, garnished with saffron, mint and crushed black pepper.

Pineapple and White Pepper Granita

A fruity semi-frozen dessert of Italian origin, granitas are a refreshing end to a meal with their icy crystalline texture and endless possibilities of variations. Oranges or grapefruit are also great flavour options.

Serves 4 to 6

Ingredients

1 cup sugar

4 tablespoons elderflower syrup

2 tablespoons crushed white pepper

2 ounces white rum

1 large ripe pineapple, peeled, cored and coarsely chopped

10 ounces fresh pineapple juice

Mint leaves for garnish

Directions

Combine sugar, white pepper and ¼ cup water in a small saucepan over medium heat and cook, stirring until the sugar dissolves. Set aside to cool. Add elderflower syrup and let the mixture rest for 30 minutes at room temperature to allow the flavours to combine.

Process the pineapple chunks, juice and elderflower syrup in a blender into a puree.

Transfer to a baking dish and freeze for at least 2 hours, scraping with a fork every 45 minutes to an hour, ensuring that the mixture is icy, aerated and fluffy. Serve garnished with mint.

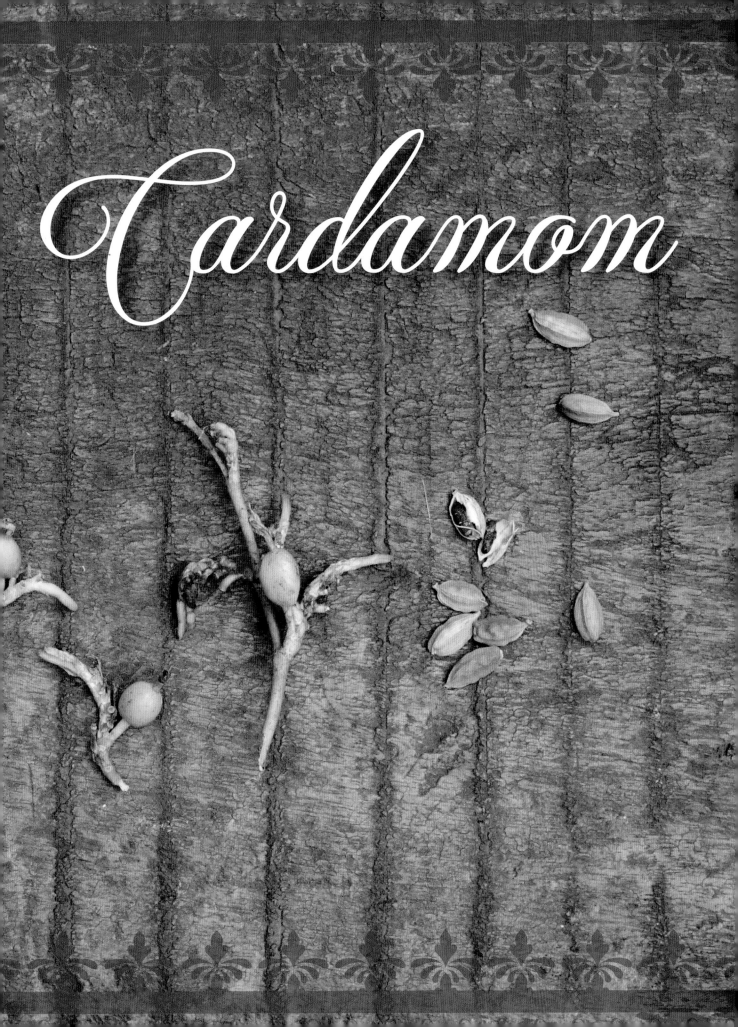

Cardamom

Cardamom

Elettaria cardamomum is the botanical name for cardamom, the queen of spices and a perennial bushy shrub, originally native to the western area of India, Pakistan, Nepal and Bhutan. Today, cardamom is grown in Central American countries such as Guatemala, Costa Rica and El Salvador, as well as in Southeast Asia—Sri Lanka, Thailand, Laos and Vietnam.

In India, cardamom has been mentioned in early Ayurvedic medical records from 1000 BC. It's generally cultivated in the country in three states—Kerala, Karnataka and Tamil Nadu.

The cardamom plant requires a tropical climate, high levels of moisture and humidity as well as shade to grow. It's a good candidate for a secondary crop in large tea and coffee plantations.

A member of the ginger family, ZINGIBERACEAE, the cardamom plant has a fleshy tuberous rhizome and narrow leaves—lances with pointed ends. In spring, white flowers blossom with bright pink or violet streaks. In the fall, these give way to the green-brown oblong or oval papery pods enclosing the tiny aromatic seeds that are the culinary treasure, which impart the flavour that's most sought-after. Harvesting occurs from October to February, with September to November being the peak time. Picking takes place every 30–40 days during these months.

The pods are picked before they are fully ripe, while they are green. Once picked, they have to be processed via washing, curing and cleaning before they are graded and packed. They are dried either on screens for up to seven days, or alternately heated and cooled in a specially constructed furnace for two to three days. Preserving the green colour of the pods is essential, as it influences the market price of the pods.

Dried pods can be stored in a cool, dark space in an airtight container for up to three years. But once ground, the cardamom should be consumed quickly, within a month or so, to ensure best flavours.

Green whole pods have the best flavour. Cardamom is an essential ingredient in spice mixes and is used as a flavouring agent in desserts, beverages, marinations, pickles, curries, pilafs, breads as well as digestives and breath fresheners alongside fennel.

Besides culinary uses, in many cultures, cardamom is used in sacred offerings. During festivals in India, cardamom is used generously in festive foods and is a key part of the flavours of celebrations. The occasion is incomplete without the delicious fragrance of cardamom marking its auspiciousness.

Cardamom Pumpkin Fall Soup

Spice-Crusted Roasted Lamb Salad

Chunky Guacamole on Toast

Buttery Apple Cider Russet Potatoes

Agave Cardamom Shrimp

Green Peas Creamy Risotto

Grapefruit Ginger Medley

Banana Fritters with Cardamom Sugar

Cardamom Pumpkin Fall Soup

As fall descends and I walk by the supermarket, boxes filled with varieties of squashes in beautiful colours and shapes beckon, and I rush to try out recipes that make the most of these special gifts of the season. I make a large batch of pumpkin soup that I can heat up at short notice and serve with nice crusty bread. This recipe is a special favourite, rich and warm with flavours of cardamom.

Serves 4

Ingredients

2 tablespoons unsalted butter

1 medium red onion, finely chopped

2 cloves garlic, chopped

2 cups yellow pumpkin, peeled, seeded and diced

1 teaspoon turmeric powder

1 teaspoon coarsely ground cardamom seeds, plus more for garnish

1 green chilli, such as serrano, split

Salt to taste

4 cups vegetable stock

3 tablespoons heavy cream

Directions

Heat the butter in a saucepan over medium heat. Add onion and garlic, stirring continuously until the onion begins to caramelise around the edges, about 4 to 5 minutes.

Add pumpkin, turmeric, cardamom, green chilli and salt and cook until the pumpkin is evenly coated with flavours. Add the vegetable stock, increase the heat to high and bring to a boil.

Reduce the heat, cover and simmer until the pumpkin is very tender, about 3 to 4 minutes.

Remove and transfer to a blender. Cautiously process to a fine puree.

Strain and add back to the saucepan. Add heavy cream and cook to desired consistency, about 3 to 4 minutes. Adjust seasoning to taste.

Garnish with crushed cardamom and serve hot with crusty bread.

Spice-Crusted Roasted Lamb Salad

This is an impressive, warm and moist lamb salad infused with the wonderful aromas of cardamom, cinnamon and fennel. Tossed with peppery rucola leaves, tomatoes and caramelised onions, this is a perfectly delicious start to a special evening.

Serves 4 to 6

Ingredients

6 to 8 cardamom pods

1-inch cinnamon stick

2 star anise

1 teaspoon cumin seeds

1 teaspoon black peppercorns

1 teaspoon fennel seeds

1 teaspoon cayenne pepper

Salt to taste

4 tablespoons vegetable or canola oil

Juice of 2 lemons

1 (about 6 to 7 pounds) boneless leg of lamb

1 medium red onion, thinly sliced

Pinch of sugar

½ cup rucola leaves, rinsed and dried

1 medium ripe tomato, sliced

Directions

Preheat the oven to 150°F.

On a sheet pan, lay out the cardamom, cinnamon, star anise, cumin, black peppercorns and fennel. Dry-roast in the oven for 8 to 10 minutes until fragrant. Remove and let cool at room temperature.

Transfer to a spice grinder and process to a fine powder.

Strain the mixture into a mixing bowl. Reserve ½ teaspoon of spice mixture.

Add cayenne pepper, salt, oil and juice of 1 lemon to the remaining spice blend and mix well.

Preheat the oven to 350°F.

Pat the lamb dry, score the fat by making ½-inch by ¼-inch cuts all over with the tip of a paring knife.

Place the lamb in a lightly oiled roasting pan. Evenly rub it with the spice paste using your hands. Marinate for 25 to 30 minutes.

Roast the lamb for about 1½ hours, until tender and cooked through. Transfer the lamb to a cutting board and let it rest for 15 to 20 minutes before carving.

Heat remaining oil in a skillet over medium heat. Add onion and sugar and cook until the onion begins to caramelise. Remove from heat.

In a mixing bowl, combine the carved lamb, caramelised onion, the remaining lemon juice, rucola leaves and tomatoes. Sprinkle with the reserved spice mixture and toss gently together. Serve.

Chunky Guacamole on Toast

Guacamole is the perfect topping anytime and this chunky version has the unique and intense flavouring of cardamom that gives it a rich, delicious edge.

An instant crowd-pleaser, including a guacamole recipe in your menu is always a good idea. Preferably choose small, ripe Hass avocados and fresh cilantro and blend into a chunky consistency. Make fresh right before serving to avoid oxidation from settling in.

Serves 4

Ingredients

½ teaspoon butter

1 loaf crusty bread, preferably sourdough, sliced

2 cloves garlic

2 tablespoons olive oil

2 ripe avocados, peeled, pitted and lightly mashed

1 medium tomato, coarsely chopped

1 red onion, finely chopped

¼ cup cilantro, finely chopped

1 jalapeño, minced

Juice of 2 limes

½ teaspoon salt, or to taste

½ teaspoon cardamom powder

Directions

Heat a griddle pan over high heat, add butter and toast a bread slice, about 2 minutes on each side, until nice and crusty.

Remove from heat, rub with fresh garlic and set aside. Repeat with remaining slices.

In a large bowl, combine all the remaining ingredients and mix gently to form a creamy consistency.

Spoon the guacamole over the garlic bread slices and serve immediately.

Buttery Apple Cider Russet Potatoes

Robust and firm, russet potatoes work well for these tender and succulent potato rounds. Fatty butter and grapeseed oil are necessary to fry the potatoes to a nice crisp, and the cider helps cook them through, while adding a refreshing sourness to the dish.

Serves 4 to 6

Ingredients

6 medium russet potatoes

2 tablespoons grapeseed oil

3 to 4 cardamom pods, lightly crushed

4 cloves garlic, minced

½ cup butter

1 cup apple cider

Salt to taste

Directions

Peel the potatoes, trim the ends and cut up into ¾ to 1-inch-size thick round slices, which helps in even cooking.

Heat grapeseed oil in a large heavy-bottom skillet over medium heat. Add the cardamom pods and garlic, and cook until fragrant. Add the butter and heat till it becomes frothy.

Place potatoes in the butter in a single layer. Cook, turning occasionally, until evenly browned on both sides. Add apple cider, reduce heat to low. Add salt and cook until the potatoes are cooked through and the liquid evaporates, about 10 minutes.

Agave Cardamom Shrimp

Agave syrup adds a sweet depth and perfectly balances the complex and exotic cardamom, and fragrant and tart red wine vinegar. Grilling the shrimp with the shell to golden perfection keeps it moist and tender within.

Serves 4

Ingredients

1½ pounds large shrimp

4 tablespoons olive oil, plus more for greasing

2 tablespoons agave syrup

2 tablespoons red wine vinegar

6 to 8 cardamom pods, lightly crushed

Salt to taste

Fresh herbs for garnish

Directions

Trim the shrimp shells with scissors down the middle of the back. Leave the tail and the first segment of the shell untouched. To devein, make a cut along the length of the back, making sure to leave the back intact.

Whisk all the ingredients together except for the shrimp in a mixing bowl. Add the shrimp and toss gently to coat well. Marinate at room temperature for 10 to 15 minutes.

Grease and heat a grilling pan over medium heat. Add the shrimp and cook, turning once, until golden and cooked through. This will take about 2 to 3 minutes each side, depending on the size of the shrimp.

Garnish with fresh herbs and serve with a salad of your choice.

Green Peas Creamy Risotto

For this creamy risotto with just the right bite, high-starch rice like Arborio is necessary to get the right consistency. There are numerous risotto variations, but the green peas and cardamom make this a side that pairs very well with meat and chicken dishes.

Serves 4

Ingredients

3 cups chicken stock

1 bay leaf

1 teaspoon black peppercorns

1-inch cinnamon stick

1 tablespoon unsalted butter

1 tablespoon olive oil

2 shallots, finely chopped

1 cup uncooked Arborio rice

1 teaspoon cardamom seeds, crushed

½ cup peas, thawed (if frozen)

¼ cup Parmesan cheese

Juice of 1 lemon

Salt to taste

Directions

In a large saucepan, combine the chicken stock, bay leaf, black peppercorns and cinnamon. Strain and keep warm on low heat.

In a heavy-bottom saucepan, heat butter and olive oil over medium heat. Add the shallots, rice and cardamom and cook until fragrant and translucent, about 3 to 4 minutes.

Add the stock mixture to the rice, a ladle at a time, stirring constantly, allowing the rice to absorb the stock in between the additions. Cook until the rice is al dente, about 15 to 20 minutes.

Add the peas, cheese and lemon juice. Season with salt and serve immediately with olives and salad.

Grapefruit Ginger Medley

The alluring flavour of cardamom lends itself well to the sweet-tart juice of grapefruit, along with the orangey notes of Angostura bitters.

Serves 4

Ingredients

3 cups ruby red grapefruit juice

Pinch of ground cardamom

Dash of Angostura bitters

1 teaspoon ginger juice

1 teaspoon honey

Directions

Combine all the ingredients in a pitcher and mix well. Pour into glasses over crushed ice.

Banana Fritters with Cardamom Sugar

These golden, crispy delicious banana fritters are hard to resist and very addictive. Sprinkled with cardamom sugar, these sweet favourites are best eaten warm and fresh.

Serves 4

Ingredients

½ cup all-purpose flour

½ cup whole wheat flour

2 tablespoons sugar

¼ teaspoon baking powder

Pinch of salt

1 large egg, lightly beaten

½ teaspoon sandalwood extract

Vegetable oil, for deep-frying

4 bananas, ripe yet firm

2 tablespoons confectioner's sugar

1 tablespoon ground cardamom

Directions

In a large mixing bowl, combine the flours, sugar, baking powder, salt, egg, sandalwood extract and ¾ to 1 cup water, and mix until a pancake-batter consistency is reached.

In a wok, heat oil to about 350°F.

Peel the bananas and cut them into 3 to 4 pieces each. Dip into the batter to coat evenly and deep-fry, turning occasionally until golden, 2 to 3 minutes.

Remove with a slotted spoon and drain on paper towels.

In a small mixing bowl, combine the confectioner's sugar and cardamom powder.

Place the fritters on a serving plate, sprinkle with cardamom sugar and serve warm with the ice cream of your choice.

Cinnamon

Cinnamon

Cinnamomum zeylanicum

History is filled with references to this warm aromatic spice—the dried bark of several evergreen trees that are part of the Cinnamomum species, which curl up when dry to form the distinct shape of cinnamon sticks. The two main kinds of cinnamon are true cinnamon, also known as Ceylon cinnamon, which is native to Sri Lanka—is expensive and difficult to find. The other kind, which is commercially available, is cassia, scientifically called Cinnamomum cassia or Cinnamomum aromaticaum.

There are several hundred varieties but cassia (Chinese) cinnamon, Saigon (Vietnam) cinnamon and Korintje (Indonesia) are grouped together as the cassia variety. Dark-coloured cassia is spicy, pungent and stronger than the light brown Ceylon cinnamon, which is mildly sweet. The aromas too are intense and pungent in cassia versus the sweet aromatic Ceylon cinnamon. The main oil in cinnamon is cinnamaldehyde. The presence of eugenol in true cinnamon is a key difference, giving it a hint of clove-like flavour, which is absent in cassia cinnamon.

One of the world's most in-demand commodities, cinnamon has a multitude of uses—as a spice and seasoning, for preserving food and for medicinal purposes. Egyptians are believed to have used cinnamon for embalming and as an anointing oil, as per the Old Testament.

It is not known exactly where cinnamon came from, though it is believed by Europeans to have shipped from ports of Egypt. Stories tell of cinnamon being gathered by mythological birds; some say it was gathered from deep canyons guarded by snakes.

The search for spice routes opened the path for the discovery of the New World. Cinnamon was heavily in demand when Christopher Columbus set sail on an adventure that changed the world. He believed he had found cinnamon and sent it back from the New World, but the cinnamon-growing country was yet to be discovered.

Finally, the Portuguese were able to find cinnamon in Ceylon, now Sri Lanka, conquered the area to gain exclusive control of the spice and retained it for a century. The Dutch took it from there for the next 150 years until the British took over in 1784. In 1800, cinnamon began to be cultivated in other regions and therefore lost its precious commodity status.

Ceylon cinnamon is grown in Sri Lanka, Brazil, India, Madagascar and the Caribbean and is used in Europe, South Asia, Africa, Mexico and Latin America. It has less coumarin than cassia, which is considered better for health. Most of the cinnamon available in the US is the cassia or Korintje.

Sri Lanka produces up to 90 per cent of Ceylon cinnamon, while Indonesia is the major producer of the other variety along with China, India and Vietnam.

After the evergreen tree's soft bark has grown for about two years, it is cut down to ground level. From the tree stump, new trees grow the following year. Generally, harvesting takes place twice a year after the rains.

The outer bark of the cut trees is scraped off, and the branch is beaten evenly with a hammer. Once the inner bark is loosened, it is carefully removed into long rolls. The cinnamon strips are dried within four to six hours, whereby they curl into quills. They are then cut into smaller quills for sale, about 2–4 inches each. The cinnamon is graded on the basis of the diameter of the quills and the number per kilogramme.

Featherings are small pieces of bark that cannot be converted into quills. The lowest grade is the chips or shavings. Both these grades are used for obtaining ground cinnamon. The lighter the colour of cinnamon, the higher the quality. Ground cinnamon loses its flavour fast so should be bought in small quantities. Cinnamon sticks will stay for up to three years in an airtight container.

The beloved warm and spicy flavour and woody aroma enhances dishes the world over—desserts, baked goods, breads, condiments, curries, meat, vegetables and beverages. It pairs particularly well with chocolate and apples. Cinnamon is also essential to spice mixes and blends.

Comforting Chicken Vegetable Soup

Anchovy and Ginger-Infused Warm Salad

Peach Cider Poached Chicken Sandwich

Apricot and Honey Lamb Stew

Orange Blossom Pilaf with Strawberries

Minty Gooseberry Cinnamonade

Persimmon Strudel

Comforting Chicken Vegetable Soup

Broth-based soups are light and versatile, and can be loaded with ingredients of your choice. Quick and easy to whip up, these soups are a great option for losing weight.

Serves 4

Ingredients

4 cups chicken stock

2 chicken breasts, cut into strips

1 cup orange juice

2 tablespoons rice vinegar

2-inch cinnamon stick

1 teaspoon allspice

3 to 4 dried kaffir lime leaves

1 teaspoon white pepper

Salt to taste

1 cup green peas, thawed (if frozen)

1 red pepper, seeded and cut into strips

Directions

In a large saucepan, bring stock, chicken, orange juice, vinegar, cinnamon, allspice, kaffir lime leaves, white pepper and salt to a boil over high heat. Reduce heat to low, cover and simmer until the chicken is cooked through, about 10 to 15 minutes. Occasionally skim the froth that appears on the surface of the soup.

Add peas and red pepper and continue to simmer for 4 to 5 minutes, until the flavours are well combined.

Serve hot.

Anchovy and Ginger-Infused Warm Salad

Roasting vegetables and fruits is a great way to cook them; it makes them crisp, succulent and flavourful. Spread them out on a baking sheet to cook evenly.

Serves 4

Ingredients

1 tablespoon olive oil

2 anchovy fillets, packed in oil, drained and finely chopped

1 shallot, minced

2 cloves garlic, minced

1-inch piece of ginger, minced

1 teaspoon lemon rind

1 teaspoon cinnamon

Salt to taste

½ teaspoon white pepper

½ fennel bulb, cut into small pieces

6 golden carrots, peeled and thinly sliced

8 to 10 red radish, quartered

¼ cup spoon tomatoes

2 star fruit, sliced

1 red apple, thinly sliced

2 tablespoons coarsely chopped dill leaves

Directions

Preheat the oven to 375°F.

In a small mixing bowl, combine oil, anchovies, shallot, garlic, ginger, lemon rind, cinnamon, salt and white pepper. Mix well and set aside.

In a large mixing bowl, combine all the fruits and vegetables with the anchovy dressing and toss to coat well.

Spread out on a baking sheet in a single layer and roast until aromatic and cooked, about 10 to 15 minutes. Turn occasionally to ensure even cooking.

Garnish with chopped dill and serve warm.

Peach Cider Poached Chicken Sandwich

It is the perfect filling—chicken poached in peach cider, warm cinnamon and Dijon mustard to melting tenderness—tossed in hung yogurt. Fish and turkey are also good options for this sandwich or wrap, and on their own in a salad.

Serves 4

Ingredients

2 cups peach cider, or as required

1 teaspoon Dijon mustard

1 teaspoon cinnamon powder

Salt to taste

4 chicken breasts, cut into 1-inch cubes

½ cup hung or Greek yogurt

2 tablespoons finely chopped parsley

12 multigrain bread slices

8 to 10 lettuce leaves

1 tomato, sliced

Fried eggs for garnish

Directions

In a medium saucepan, combine peach cider, Dijon mustard, cinnamon powder, salt and chicken cubes and bring to a boil. Reduce the heat to medium and simmer until the mixture is dry, about 12 to 15 minutes. Remove from heat and bring to room temperature.

In a mixing bowl, combine the chicken, hung yogurt and parsley, and season with salt if required.

To build the sandwich, layer a slice of bread with lettuce, tomato and chicken salad and top with a fried egg. Repeat with the remaining ingredients and serve.

Apricot and Honey Lamb Stew

Tender lamb is enriched with a warm sweet-spicy flavour when cooked with apricot, orange juice and honey. This recipe is similar to stews cooked in tagines in the Middle East. The warming aroma of cinnamon is the highlight of this dish.

Serves 4

Ingredients

1 cup apricot puree

1 tablespoon honey

Salt to taste

1 tablespoon chilli powder

½ cup orange juice

4 tablespoons vegetable oil

1 red onion, finely chopped

3 cloves garlic, minced

2-inch cinnamon stick

3 pounds lamb stew meat preferably from the shoulder, trimmed of excess fat and cut into 2-inch cubes

1 cup tomato puree

4 cups beef or chicken stock

Directions

In a mixing bowl, combine apricot puree, honey, salt, chilli powder, orange juice and 2 tablespoons of oil. Reserve.

Heat the remaining oil in a heavy-bottom pan over medium heat. Add the onion, garlic and cinnamon and cook until the onion begins to caramelise, about 5 to 8 minutes. Add the lamb and salt and sear until lightly browned, about 3 to 4 minutes, stirring continuously. Pour in the apricot mixture along with the tomato puree and continue to cook until the liquid dries up.

Add stock and bring to a boil. Reduce heat to low, cover and simmer until the flavours are well combined, and the lamb is tender and cooked through, about 30 to 40 minutes. Add more stock if required.

Serve hot with couscous and salad of your choice.

Orange Blossom Pilaf with Strawberries

Pilaf has Middle Eastern roots and is typically cooked in a seasoned broth. Sweet strawberry and cool spearmint fill each fluffy mouthful of this pilaf with bursts of flavour, echoing with the scent of orange blossom.

Serves 4

Ingredients

2 tablespoons vegetable oil

2 cups basmati rice, rinsed and drained

Salt to taste

2-inch cinnamon stick

4 cups vegetable stock

1 teaspoon orange blossom

1 lemon rind

1 cup strawberries, hulled and sliced

Spearmint for garnish

Directions

Heat oil in a saucepan over medium heat. Stir in rice, salt and cinnamon and cook stirring constantly until the rice becomes translucent, about 2 minutes. Add stock, orange blossom and lemon rind and bring to a boil. Continue to cook until the stock is absorbed, about 12 to 15 minutes.

Place a damp kitchen towel over the pan, cover with a lid, reduce the heat to low and cook for another 3 to 4 minutes until every grain of rice is cooked. Toss in the strawberries, garnish with spearmint and serve.

Minty Gooseberry Cinnamonade

The use of cinnamon has been recorded since ancient times, its unique aroma and sweet taste uplifted the flavour of recipes such as this drink. Golden cape gooseberries jazz up the drink with their sweet-and-sour taste.

Serves 4 to 6

Ingredients

Eight 1-inch cinnamon sticks

1 cup sugar

½ teaspoon mint essence

Juice of 3 lemons, or to taste

16 to 20 golden cape gooseberries, hulled and sliced

Mint leaves for garnish

Directions

In a small saucepan, combine 2 cinnamon sticks, sugar and ½ cup water and cook stirring until the sugar is dissolved. Remove from heat and add the mint essence. Let the flavours steep while cooling to room temperature.

Transfer the syrup to a pitcher, add lemon juice and top with seltzer water. Garnish with gooseberries, mint and the remaining cinnamon sticks.

Persimmon Strudel

A bite of warm cinnamon-flavoured flaky crusted persimmon strudel is perfect by itself or paired with cream or a scoop of ice cream. Leftovers can be stored in the refrigerator for up to five days.

Serves 4

Ingredients

6 ripe but firm Fuyu persimmons

2 teaspoons cinnamon powder

½ cup sugar

Juice of ½ lemon

Pinch of salt

½ cup lightly roasted hazelnuts, coarsely chopped

8 phyllo sheets (roughly 13 by 16 inches), thawed (if frozen)

1 stick unsalted butter, melted, or as required

Directions

Preheat the oven to 375°F.

Line a baking sheet with parchment paper.

Slice off persimmon tops and cut into cubes. Place in a mixing bowl and toss with 1 teaspoon cinnamon powder, sugar, lemon juice and salt.

Transfer to a saucepan on medium heat. Add hazelnuts and cook, stirring constantly, until the mixture becomes thick, about 3 to 4 minutes.

Remove from heat and bring to room temperature.

Place a phyllo sheet on a working surface. Brush with melted butter. Layer with another sheet and brush with butter again. Repeat to layer 6 phyllo sheets.

Place the persimmon filling on the prepared sheets, leaving a ½-inch border on one side. Starting with the long end, roll to enclose filling, tucking in the ends too. Brush the top of the roll with butter and place on the baking sheet.

Place the remaining 2 phyllo sheets on the work surface. Grease them and cut into thin strips.

Place the strips over the persimmon-filled roll and bake until golden brown, for 40 to 50 minutes.

In a small mixing bowl, combine 2 tablespoons confectioner's sugar and the remaining cinnamon powder.

Dust the strudel with this mixture and serve warm.

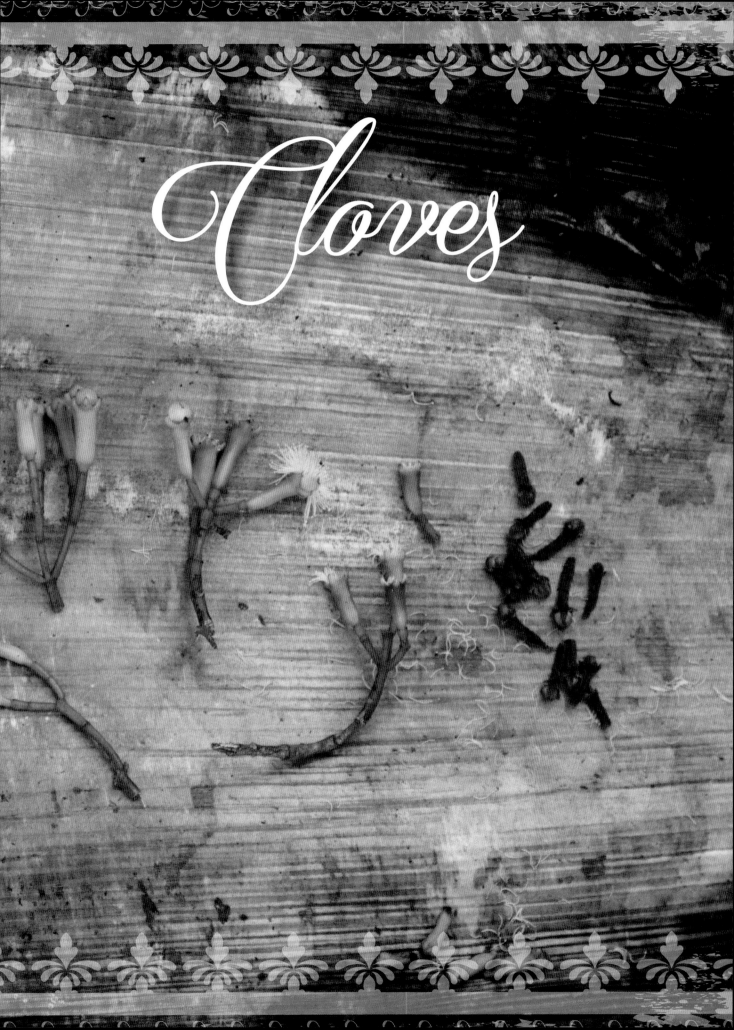

Cloves

Clove

The aromatic clove, *Syzygium aromaticum*, is the flower bud of a small tropical evergreen tree used as a spice in cuisines worldwide. It is native to the Molucca Islands or Spice Islands in Indonesia. According to tradition, people on these islands use clove trees when they wanted to celebrate the arrival of a new member into their family. Cloves are commercially produced there as well as in Bangladesh, India, Pakistan, Sri Lanka and Tanzania.

The clove tree is part of the myrtle family capable of surviving in the wild for several hundred years; it thrives in coastal areas, and its trunks can reach heights between 12 and 40 feet. It has large oval and shiny aromatic leaves, dark green and growing in pairs, while its small flowers are arranged in terminal clusters—they grow at the end of branches or stems. Initially pale in colour, the flower buds turn green and eventually a bright red when they are ready for harvesting. Being a hermaphrodite—plants with both stamens and pistils in the flower—bees help in pollination as they are attracted to the flowers because of the sweet smell, which comes from eugenol, an essential oil in cloves. The brown fruit, known as the mother clove, is berry-like Druze containing one seed.

The tree is in bloom from July to September, from November to January. When the buds are less than 2 cm and have matured to reddish pink, they are hand-picked.

If in clusters, they are carefully separated and spread out for sun-drying for up to five days. The bud turns brown while the stem is a dark reddish-brown.

Cloves can be used whole or ground and have been a spice and flavouring in cuisines of Asia, the Middle East and Africa. They go into marinades, curries, beverages and spice blends, and thrive as a pickling or mulling spice. A small quantity of cloves goes a long way in imparting flavour thanks to eugenol—hot peppery notes, sharp and bitter, leaving a numbing sensation in the mouth.

The clove tree is believed to be the oldest in the world, approximately 400 years old. Historical references have been found regarding cloves from the Han Dynasty, the Middle Ages and *Arabian Nights*. In Ayurvedic and Chinese medicine, herbalism, dentistry and aromatherapy, cloves have been prized for their warm, aromatic qualities, which act as a painkiller and help with several ailments. Embedded into an orange, it becomes a pomander, which, in Victorian England, was considered a warm gift for wishes of good fortune.

Charred Carrot and Galangal Soup

Spice-Poached Pears with Braised Cabbage

Roasted Garlic and Cannellini on Toast

Yuzu-Maple Pan Seared Chicken

Almond Milk and Rose-Scented Basmati Rice

Jaggery and Chickpea Flatbread

Spicy Blood Orange Cooler

Chia Seeds in Coconut Cream

Charred Carrot and Galangal Soup

Charring carrots gives a taste edge that overall enriches this soup, while sweet potatoes not only help to thicken it but also provide a creamy texture. From the ginger family, there's galangal, which has an aromatic and spicy bite that works well here.

Serves 4

Ingredients

Oil for greasing, plus 1 tablespoon vegetable oil

3 to 4 medium carrots, peeled and chopped

1 tablespoon unsalted butter

1 red onion, finely chopped

2 cloves garlic, minced

1 sweet potato, peeled and diced

3 cups vegetable stock

1 teaspoon ground cloves

½ teaspoon smoked paprika

1-inch fresh galangal, minced

Salt to taste

1 teaspoon red chilli powder

Directions

Heat a grill pan over high heat and grease lightly. Place the carrots and lightly char. Remove from heat and set aside.

Heat the butter in a saucepan over medium heat. Add the onion and garlic, and sauté until the onion is translucent, 2 to 3 minutes. Add the charred carrots and sweet potato and continue to cook, stirring, for about a minute.

Add stock, ½ teaspoon clove powder, paprika, galangal and salt and bring to a boil over high heat. Reduce heat to low, cover and simmer until the potato is cooked and the mixture becomes little thick.

Remove from heat and transfer to a blender. Process until smooth. Keep warm.

Heat 1 tablespoon oil in a small skillet over medium heat, then remove from heat and add chilli powder and the remaining clove powder.

Ladle the soup into bowls and serve drizzled with the clove-chilli oil.

Spice-Poached Pears with Braised Cabbage

Make sure to choose firm pears so that they retain their shape as they soak in the spices and red wine. Feel free to vary flavourings in the poaching liquid to create complexity and intensity as per your taste.

Serves 4

Ingredients

½ cup dry red wine

1 teaspoon cloves

1 teaspoon cinnamon

1-inch piece of ginger, minced

6 ripe Anjou pears, peeled

2 tablespoons oil

1 medium red onion, finely chopped

1 medium cabbage, quartered, cored and thinly sliced

2 tablespoons red wine vinegar

½ cup vegetable stock

Salt to taste

Freshly ground black pepper to taste

Parmesan shavings for garnish

Directions

In a medium-size pot, combine red wine, cloves, cinnamon and ginger and bring to a boil on high heat. Reduce the heat, add the pears, cover and simmer for 10 to 15 minutes, or until the pears are cooked but still firm. Drain and slice the pears. Set aside.

Heat oil in a medium saucepan over medium heat. Add onion and cook until translucent. Add the cabbage, stir and continue to cook, then add vinegar, vegetable stock, salt and pepper and cook for 10 to 12 minutes, or until the liquid has been absorbed.

Transfer the cabbage to a serving dish. Top with pear slices and shaved Parmesan and serve.

Roasted Garlic and Cannellini on Toast

A classic and simple Italian favourite, this bruschetta recipe can be easily adapted to suit the tastes and preferences of your guests. The garlicky cannellini topping is just one idea to get you started. Roasting the garlic creates a strong flavour, which is unmatched, so use as per taste. The nutty and nutritious cannellini are full of protein and fibre, and are low on fat. The beans have a silky but firm texture that holds well when mixed with lemon, olive oil and garlic. They're a good alternative to baked beans. The toppings can be made in advance and added to crisp baguette right before serving.

Serves 4

Ingredients

1 garlic head

2 tablespoons extra-virgin olive oil

1 can cannellini beans, rinsed and drained

Juice of 1 lemon

Salt to taste

½ teaspoon clove powder

2 tablespoons chopped parsley

1 French baguette, or bread of your choice

Pomegranate seeds for garnish

Directions

Preheat the oven to 400°F.

Gently remove the loose papery outer covering of the garlic and very carefully trim off ¼-inch off the top of the garlic head. Drizzle 1 tablespoon olive oil on the exposed garlic cloves, wrap in aluminium foil and roast in the oven for 30 to 40 minutes until the cloves are soft and caramelised.

Remove from the oven and carefully place the softened garlic in a mixing bowl. Add cannellini beans, lemon juice, salt, clove powder and parsley.

Cut the bread into ½ to 1-inch thick slices. Drizzle each slice with olive oil and top with the roasted garlic and cannellini mixture. Garnish with pomegranate seeds and serve.

Yuzu-Maple Pan Seared Chicken

A little clove adds an intense flavour to chicken marinated in yuzu, maple, garlic and soy sauce. Yuzu adds a deep citrus fragrance and taste.

Serves 4

Ingredients

2 tablespoons yuzu juice, plus more if required

1 tablespoon maple syrup

2 cloves garlic, minced

1 tablespoon soy sauce

1 teaspoon hot sauce of your choice, or per taste

Salt to taste

3 boneless, skinless chicken breasts, cut into thin strips

2 tablespoons oil

1 teaspoon cloves

1-inch piece of ginger, minced

1 orange, halved

Micro greens for garnish

Directions

In a mixing bowl, combine the yuzu juice, maple syrup, garlic, soy sauce, hot sauce, salt and chicken and toss gently to coat well. Let the chicken marinate in the refrigerator for about 2 hours.

Heat oil in a heavy skillet over medium heat. Add cloves and ginger and sauté for a minute until fragrant. Place the orange halves cut side down in the oil, until it caramelises. Remove and reserve for garnish.

Sear the chicken in the clove-infused oil, turning gently until cooked through. Add some yuzu juice if required.

Garnish with microgreens and serve with caramelised orange halves on the side.

Almond Milk and
Rose-Scented Basmati Rice

The invisible scent of spices is the true magic of bouquet garni, which has been used in ancient cuisines for centuries. It creates layers of flavours that coat each grain. I also make this dish using barley and quinoa. The cooking time will vary but it still tastes great.

Serves 4

Ingredients

4 to 6 cardamom

6 to 8 dried rosebuds

2 star anise

2 tablespoons oil

4 to 6 cloves

1 cup long-grain basmati rice, rinsed, soaked in water for 3 minutes and drained

1 cup almond milk

Salt to taste

Basil for garnish

Directions

Place a 10-inch square muslin cloth on a work surface. In the centre, place cardamom, rosebuds and star anise and bring the edges of the cloth together to tie with a kitchen string. Make a tight bundle.

In a large stockpot, heat oil over medium heat. Add cloves and cook for about a minute until the oil is infused. Add rice, almond milk, 1 cup water, salt and the bouquet garni and bring to a boil over high heat. Cook for 10 to 12 minutes, or until the liquid is absorbed.

Reduce heat to low, cover the rice with a damp kitchen towel, then place a lid on top. Continue to cook until the rice is cooked, about 5 to 10 minutes. Remove from heat, fluff rice with a fork and discard the bouquet garni.

Garnish with basil and serve.

Jaggery and Chickpea Flatbread

This is a very versatile recipe. The stuffing can be varied, and the bread does not require any leavening agent. The jaggery adds a beautiful caramelised flavour as it cooks.

Serves 5

Ingredients

For the dough

1 cup whole wheat flour

1 cup all-purpose flour

2 tablespoons oats

1 tablespoon oil

Salt to taste

For the filling

1 (15 ounces) can chickpeas, rinsed, drained and mashed

2 tablespoons finely grated jaggery

2 tablespoons sesame seeds

1 teaspoon clove powder

5 tablespoons clarified butter

Almond slivers for garnish

Directions

In a mixing bowl, combine the flours, oats, salt and oil and gradually add about ¾ cup water while kneading to make a semi-soft dough. Cover and let it rest for 15 minutes.

In another mixing bowl, combine mashed chickpeas, jaggery, sesame seeds and clove powder.

Divide the dough into 5 equal-size balls, then roll each out into a 4-inch disc. Place one-fifth of the chickpea mixture in the centre of the discs. Bring their edges together to enclose the filling.

Dust the work surface lightly with flour. Roll out each stuffed dough ball into 6-inch discs. Brush one side of each with clarified butter.

Heat a griddle over medium heat. Place the disc on it, butter-side down. Cook until browned and crisp, about 2 minutes. Brush the exposed top of the flatbread with clarified butter and flip the disc to cook the other side until brown and crisp, another 2 minutes. Remove from heat and keep warm. Repeat with the remaining discs.

Garnish with almond and serve warm.

Spicy Blood Orange Cooler

Orange-crimson tart blood orange juice is the base for this party favourite. The warmth of cloves and a dash of hot sauce gives it a spicy kick. Transform it into a dashing cocktail by adding liquor, such as tequila or vodka.

Serves 4 to 6

Ingredients

½ cup sugar

4 to 6 cloves

1 tablespoon honey

Pinch of salt

Blood orange juice as required

Hot sauce of your choice as required

Orange peel for garnish

Directions

In a small saucepan, combine sugar, 1 cup water, cloves, honey and a pinch of salt and stir over medium heat until the sugar dissolves. Remove from heat and let the flavours steep. Cool to room temperature.

To serve, add sugar syrup as per taste. Top with blood orange juice, a dash of hot sauce and garnish with an orange peel. Serve chilled.

Chia Seeds in Coconut Cream

Chia seeds are an energy superfood, simple to use in recipes and gluten-free. They bloom like tapioca when soaked overnight and have a pudding-like texture. Mix in flavourings and toppings of your choice.

Serves 4

Ingredients

½ cup chia seeds

Few drops vanilla essence

1 can (5.4 ounces) unsweetened coconut cream

¼ teaspoon ground cloves

5 tablespoons honey, or to taste

Freshly slivered coconut for garnish

Dried cranberries for garnish

Fresh golden cape gooseberries for garnish

Directions

In a mixing bowl, combine the chia seeds, vanilla, coconut cream, 1 cup warm water, cloves and honey and refrigerate for 3 hours, until the seeds bloom.

Stir and season with sugar if required. Divide into serving bowls, garnish with coconut, dried cranberries and fresh gooseberries, and serve.

Coriander

Coriander

This annual aromatic herb of the Apiaceae family (*Coriandrum sativum*) is native to regions of Europe, Africa and southwest Asia. The seeds are used as a spice and the leaves are widely used as a herb for garnishes. It is one of the first spices grown by early settlers and brought to North America in 1670. Coriander is also known as Chinese parsley or cilantro, which is the Spanish word for coriander.

The plant is 20-inch tall and the leaves at the base are broadly lobed. New feathery leaves grow at the higher points on the stems. White or pale pink asymmetrical flowers grow in clusters or umbels. The fruit is spherical—a schizocarp, where a dry fruit splits, when mature, into mericarps. The plant grows in dry and cool weather—June to July and October to November.

Coriander leaves can be cut usually when the plant is six inches tall, while fine new leaves are best for cooking. The leaves cannot be dried, unlike other herbs. Once the flowers appear, the plant stops producing edible leaves.

The leaves are the parts commonly known as cilantro and have a lemony aroma and delicate, refreshing flavour, with hints of mint and cloves. They are used in Indian, Chinese and Thai cooking as a garnish as well as, in chutneys and salads. In Mexican cuisine, cilantro is combined with chillies, garlic and lime juice for dressings and sauces, while in the Middle East, it goes into spice pastes. Cilantro is added before serving, as it loses flavour in heat. Rich in vitamins A, C and K, its flavour can be retained when frozen; they also lose their aroma when dried.

The dried coriander seeds, when crushed release a lemony flavour. Used whole or ground, dry-roasting the seeds elevates the aroma and flavour. It is an important ingredient in garam masala—a versatile Indian spice mix..

In parts of Europe like Germany and Central Europe, coriander seeds are used in a variety of recipes ranging from sausages to rye bread, bouillon and marinades. It also finds use in brewing beer. In North Africa, coriander seeds are used in harissa and other spice mixtures.

Cilantro—both leaves and stems are a popular addition and garnish in Indian, Spanish and Mexican recipes. The root of the coriander plant makes its way in Thai soups and curry pastes, adding a deep, intense flavour.

Cilantro leaves can be stored in a resealable bag in the refrigerator for three to four days. Whole seeds keep well while grinding them compromises flavour, so always use freshly ground coriander.

Crackling Chickpeas

Summer Tomato Salad

Creamy Spicy Yogurt

Crab in Fennel-Coriander Broth

Coriander-Crusted Chicken Roulade

Red Pepper Jasmine Pulao

Passion Fruit Coriander Drink

Strawberry and Coriander Kulfi

Crackling Chickpeas

Garlicky, spicy and hard to resist, these crispy chickpeas won't last long once they appear at the table at your party.

A basic recipe for crispy nuts that works with your choice of nuts, the flavourings too can be changed to create the profile you're interested in—salty, savoury, spicy or sweet. The nuts can be roasted for a healthier take.

Make in large batches and store in airtight containers for up to 2 to 3 weeks.

Makes about 32 ounces

Ingredients

1 cup dry chickpeas

2 cups vegetable oil

Black salt to taste

2 teaspoons garlic powder

2 tablespoons coriander seeds, finely crushed

1 teaspoon black pepper

1 tablespoon cumin powder

Pinch of cayenne pepper, optional

Directions

Soak the chickpeas in enough water to cover overnight, then drain and rinse well. Transfer to a colander to remove as much moisture as possible.

Heat oil in a medium saucepan over medium heat to 350°F. Add chickpeas and fry in batches, stirring constantly until cooked, crispy and golden brown, about 5 to 8 minutes.

Remove with a slotted spoon and drain on a paper towel.

In a mixing bowl, combine chickpeas, salt and spices. Toss to mix well then serve or store.

Summer Tomato Salad

This is a perfect recipe that does right by the bounty of summer tomatoes! It's brimming with the sunny, natural sweetness of tomatoes and balanced with vinegar, salty feta and fresh, peppery basil.

Serves 4

Ingredients

1 tablespoon coriander seeds

1 teaspoon black peppercorns

1 tablespoon champagne vinegar

2 tablespoons olive oil

Salt to taste

4 red cherry tomatoes, thinly sliced

4 yellow cherry tomatoes, thinly sliced

2 medium heirloom yellow tomatoes, thinly sliced

2 medium heirloom red tomatoes, thinly sliced

2 medium roma tomatoes, thinly sliced

Salt to taste

10 to 12 basil leaves, roughly torn

¼ cup feta cheese

Directions

In a small skillet, dry-roast the coriander seeds and black pepper, stirring constantly until fragrant, about 2 minutes. Remove from heat and coarsely grind.

In a small mixing bowl, whisk together vinegar, olive oil, salt and coriander-pepper mix.

Arrange the tomatoes on a serving platter, drizzle with the vinegar and spice dressing, top with basil and feta cheese and serve.

Creamy Spicy Yogurt

A creamy healthy yogurt-based dip that can be served with crudités, pita bread and chips, this recipe lends well to substitute spices and herbs as per your taste. Hung yogurt is a good alternative for Greek yogurt.

Serves 4

Ingredients

1 tablespoon sesame oil

1 medium onion, finely chopped

1-inch piece of ginger, minced

1 green chilli, such as serrano, minced

1 tablespoon coriander seeds, crushed

1 teaspoon turmeric

1 teaspoon cayenne pepper, or to taste

Salt to taste

1 teaspoon sugar

1 medium tomato, coarsely chopped

2 cups Greek yogurt

Fresh cilantro leaves for garnish

Directions

Heat oil in a saucepan over medium heat. Stir-fry the onion, ginger, green chilli and coriander, stirring continuously until the onion becomes translucent. Add turmeric, cayenne pepper, salt, sugar and tomatoes. Give it a stir and remove from heat. Cool at room temperature.

In a mixing bowl, combine yogurt and the tomato-onion mixture. Mix well and season with salt if required. Garnish with cilantro and serve.

Crab in Fennel-Coriander Broth

Cooking crabs may seem like a daunting task but made-at-home, fresh crabmeat is tender and succulent. In this recipe, the crab is cooked with coriander, bay leaf, fennel, garlic and onions that add their distinct flavours to this delicious dish.

Serves 4

Ingredients

2 tablespoons canola oil

1 medium onion, diced

2 carrots, peeled and diced

1 bay leaf

1 tablespoon coriander seeds, crushed

2 cloves garlic, crushed

1 small fennel bulb, coarsely chopped

4 medium-size crabs

3 cups fish stock

Salt to taste

2 sprigs baby scallion greens

Four 5-minute boiled eggs, peeled and halved

Directions

In a large stockpot, heat oil over medium heat. Add onion, carrots, bay leaf, coriander, garlic and fennel, and cook until the onion is translucent, stirring continuously. Add the crabs and sauté for 2 to 3 minutes. Add stock and salt, cover and continue to cook for about 10 to 15 minutes or until the crabs are cooked through.

Garnish with scallion greens and eggs, and serve hot.

Coriander-Crusted Chicken Roulade

Chicken roulade makes an impressive dish for a special event. This recipe rolls in a layer of spinach inside and is coated with a coriander-breadcrumb mixture for a crisp nutty outer coating. The roulade is served with a garlic-flavoured tomato sauce.

Serves 4 to 6

Ingredients

4 tablespoons peanut oil

1 medium onion, thinly sliced

2 cups coarsely chopped spinach

¼ cup coarsely chopped walnuts

Salt to taste

Freshly ground black pepper

4 cloves garlic, minced

1 medium tomato, blanched and finely chopped

½ cup tomato puree

1 cup panko breadcrumbs

2 tablespoons coriander powder

3 boneless, skinless chicken breast halves, butterflied and pounded evenly

Directions

Preheat the oven to 375°F.

Heat 2 tablespoons oil in a medium skillet over medium heat. Add onions and sauté until translucent, then add the spinach, walnuts, salt and pepper. Stir to mix well. Remove from heat and set aside.

In a separate saucepan, heat the remaining oil over medium heat. Add garlic and cook, stirring, for about a minute. Add tomatoes, tomato puree, salt and pepper, and continue to cook until the mixture becomes thick and saucy. Remove from heat and set aside.

In a food processor, pulse the panko and coriander powder.

Flatten out the chicken breasts and season with salt and pepper. Divide the spinach mixture between them, spreading it evenly and leaving a ½-inch border all around. Roll and tie with kitchen twine. Sprinkle with the panko-coriander mixture, pressing to coat evenly.

Transfer the roulades to a greased baking sheet and bake until golden, about 30 minutes.

Serve hot on a bed of tomato-garlic sauce.

Red Pepper Jasmine Pulao

Coriander and serrano chilli complement the buttery and floral flavours of jasmine rice, tossed with paneer and red peppers. Though easy to make at home, paneer is readily available in speciality stores. Firm tofu is a good substitutes for paneer.

Serves 2

Ingredients

1 cup jasmine rice

Salt to taste

1 red pepper, seeded and diced

8 ounces paneer, cut into cubes

2 tablespoons coriander seeds, lightly roasted and crushed

1 green chilli, such as serrano, chopped

Chives for garnish

Directions

In a saucepan with a tight-fitting lid, combine rice, 2 cups of water and salt and bring to a boil on high heat. Add the red pepper, paneer, coriander and serrano, stir once and cover.

Reduce the heat to low and simmer for about 8 to 10 minutes. Remove and let it stand to absorb all the flavours, for another 5 minutes.

Gently fluff the rice with a fork, garnish with chives and serve hot.

Passion Fruit Coriander Drink

A tropical refresher with sweet pineapple and bright, ripe passion fruit. Coriander is a lemony, spicy complement to the freshness of this drink.

Serves 4

Ingredients

4 ripe passion fruit

1 cup sugar

2 tablespoons coriander seeds, lightly crushed, plus more for garnish

½ vanilla bean, split

2 star anise

3 cups pineapple juice

Directions

Cut the passion fruit, remove the pulp and reserve for use.

In a saucepan, combine sugar and ½ cup water. Add coriander, vanilla and star anise and cook on medium heat till the sugar dissolves. Remove from heat, cover and let the flavours steep for about 30 minutes. Strain and set aside.

In a pitcher, combine the passion fruit pulp and pineapple juice. Add seltzer water and sugar syrup. Cover and refrigerate. Serve over crushed ice, garnished with crushed coriander.

Strawberry and Coriander Kulfi

The classic and much-loved strawberry flavour is highlighted in this simple kulfi recipe. Crushed coriander is the unexpected element that adds a light floral note. You can use any other berries for this recipe like raspberries or blackberries.

Serves 4

Ingredients

4 cups whole milk

1 tablespoon coriander seeds, crushed

¼ cup sweetened condensed milk

1 cup fresh strawberry pulp

1 teaspoon rose extract

Directions

In a large saucepan, heat the milk and coriander over medium heat, stirring continuously until it's reduced to one-third of the original quantity. Strain and pour the milk back into the same pan.

Add condensed milk and continue to cook on medium heat for another 2 minutes. Remove from heat and cool at room temperature. Once cool, refrigerate to chill.

Stir in the strawberry pulp and 1 teaspoon rose extract and mix thoroughly. Transfer the mixture to a container, cover and freeze overnight or until ready to use.

Curry Leaves

Curry Leaves

The tropical curry tree (*Murraya koenigii* or *Bergera koenigii*) is native to India and Sri Lanka. These curry tree leaves, are used extensively in the cuisines of these two countries as well as elsewhere.

The aromatic leaves of the curry tree are pinnate, arranged on either side of the stem. Small white flowers produce berry-shaped fruit, small and shining black, containing a large single seed and edible pulp. However, neither the seed nor pulp are used in cooking.

The leaves can be picked most times of the year. They are packed in small bundles and shipped fresh. Vacuum-drying helps maintain aroma and colour.

The leaves are used in Sri Lankan food as well as India's south and western coastal cuisines, in curries and other regional recipes. In Cambodia, the leaves are toasted or roasted to crispness before being added to soup, whereas in India, the leaves are fried with other spices in the beginning or are tempered and added in the end. Crushing or chopping the leaves before adding to chutneys, relishes and marinades is a common practice. Curry leaves are just beginning to be used in Western cooking; they lend a warm lemony and slightly bitter taste and a musky aroma to dishes.

Fresh curry leaves do not keep well for long, not even in the refrigerator. Dried leaves are available but are less aromatic; however, the plant can be grown at home and fresh leaves used as needed.

The leaves are also important in Ayurveda, and the aroma finds its way into fragrances, potpourri, air fresheners, massage oils, aromatherapy products, incense, etc. During Indian rituals, curry leaves are used for prayer ceremonies too.

Crispy Chennai Chicken

Lemony Crayfish Congee

Warm Chickpea, Eggplant and
Coconut Salad

Lime-Scented Sole

Elderflower Pilaf with Baby Lobsters

Beetroot and Cherry Tomato Poriyal

Curry Leaf, Vodka and Sour Lime

Crispy Chennai Chicken

A dish from southern India—Chennai—its star ingredient is red chillies, which add fiery colour and taste to this spicy fried chicken. A pinch of asafoetida goes a long way in imparting a warm garlicky-onion taste.

Serves 4 to 6

Ingredients

2 tablespoons vegetable oil, plus more for frying

10 to 12 fresh curry leaves

1 teaspoon turmeric powder

½ teaspoon freshly ground black pepper

1 teaspoon red chilli powder, or to taste

1 teaspoon garlic powder

Pinch of asafoetida

1 teaspoon coriander seeds, lightly crushed

4 tablespoons rice flour

1 teaspoon salt

Juice of 1 lemon

3 boneless, skinless chicken breasts, cut into thin strips

Directions

In a small skillet, heat 2 tablespoons of oil on medium-high heat. Add the curry leaves and fry until fragrant. Remove from oil using a slotted spoon and drain on a paper towel. Reserve.

Transfer the infused oil to a large mixing bowl. Add the turmeric, black pepper, red chilli powder, garlic powder, asafoetida, coriander, rice flour and salt. Add lemon juice and enough water to form a pancake-batter consistency.

Add the chicken pieces and mix to coat well. Cover and allow to marinate in the refrigerator for 2 hours.

Heat the oil to 350°F. Fry the chicken in batches until golden and crisp. Remove with a slotted spoon and drain.

Serve hot and fresh, garnished with a dip of your choice.

Lemony Crayfish Congee

Congee is an Asian rice porridge-like soup, and preparations vary depending on culture and traditions. It can be served as a plain rice gruel or with chicken, meat or seafood as in this recipe. The buttery-garlicky flavours are absorbed beautifully in the crayfish meat.

Serves 4 to 6

Ingredients

1 cup short-grain rice

8 to 10 fresh curry leaves

1-inch piece of ginger, minced

1 teaspoon white pepper

Salt to taste

2 cloves garlic, minced

6 to 8 fresh crayfish tails

Juice of 1 lemon or to taste

Directions

In a stockpot, combine rice with 3 cups of water, curry leaves, ginger, white pepper and salt and bring to a boil on high heat. Reduce heat to low and simmer for about 12 to 15 minutes until the rice gets a porridge-like consistency. Remove from heat and keep warm.

Heat butter in a medium-size skillet over medium heat. Add garlic and salt and sauté for about a minute. Add the crayfish and stir occasionally until the meat is just cooked through, about 3 to 5 minutes.

Stir in the lemon juice and mix well.

Serve it hot on top of cooked rice.

Warm Chickpea, Eggplant and Coconut Salad

The delicious flavour of tempered mustard seeds and curry leaves complement the sweetness of grated coconut. Besides chickpeas, this recipe can be used with any dry legume—peas, kidney beans or even lentils—making for a light and healthy lunch or side.

Serves 4 to 6

Ingredients

4 Japanese eggplants, thinly sliced

1 teaspoon ground fennel

Salt to taste

Juice of 1 lemon

2 tablespoons olive oil, plus more for greasing

2 tablespoons vegetable oil

1 teaspoon mustard seeds

8 to 10 fresh curry leaves

1 (15 ounces) can chickpeas, rinsed and drained

4 to 6 cherry tomatoes

¼ cup freshly grated coconut

Freshly ground black pepper

2 tablespoons coarsely chopped fresh cilantro

Directions

In a large mixing bowl, combine the eggplant, fennel, salt, lemon juice and olive oil and toss to coat well.

Heat a grilling pan on medium-high heat and grease lightly. Grill the eggplant slices until slightly charred and cooked through, about 2 to 3 minutes each side. Remove from heat and set aside.

Heat oil in a medium pan over medium heat. Add mustard seeds and let them sputter, about a minute, before adding the curry leaves. Cook for another minute, then add the chickpeas, tomatoes, coconut, salt and pepper, stirring for 2 to 3 minutes.

Toss in the eggplant, garnish with cilantro and serve hot.

Lime-Scented Sole

Shallow-frying gives the sole a nice brown crust and flaky texture. As curry leaves are added to hot oil, they lend a deep citrusy flavour and aroma to the dish.

Serves 4

Ingredients

3 large silver sole or flounder, cleaned, gutted and washed

1 teaspoon curry powder

Salt to taste

1 teaspoon lime zest

2 tablespoons vegetable or canola oil, plus more if required

10 to 12 curry leaves, coarsely chopped

2 to 3 cloves garlic, minced

Pinch of asafoetida

Juice of 1 lemon, or to taste

Directions

Gently pat the fish dry and rub it with curry powder, salt and lime zest.

Set aside for at least 10 minutes for the flavours to merge.

Heat oil in a large skillet over medium heat. Add curry leaves, garlic and asafoetida and cook for a minute, until fragrant. Place the fish in a single layer in the oil and cook for 2 to 3 minutes on each side, or until it is cooked through and opaque.

Place on a serving platter and drizzle with freshly squeezed lemon juice.

Elderflower Pilaf with Baby Lobsters

This is a simple elderflower and curry leaf-flavoured pilaf, and baked lobsters rubbed with turmeric, garam masala and lemon juice. Baking is a great way to preserve the sweet taste of lobster meat—a wonderful start to an evening of entertainment.

Serves 4

Ingredients

4 baby lobsters

1 teaspoon turmeric

½ teaspoon garam masala

Salt to taste

1-inch piece of ginger, minced

3 tablespoons vegetable oil

Juice of 1 lemon

1 red onion, finely chopped

2 cloves garlic, minced

4-5 curry leaves

2 cups fish stock

Few drops elderflower essence

1 cup long-grain basmati rice

Directions

Preheat the oven to 375°F.

Cut the baby lobsters into half.

In a large mixing bowl, combine the lobster, turmeric, garam masala, salt, ginger, 1 tablespoon of oil and lemon juice and mix to coat well. Let this marinate for about 10 to 12 minutes.

Place the lobster on a lightly greased baking sheet and bake for 10 to 12 minutes, until cooked through.

In a large pan that comes with a tight lid, heat oil on medium heat. Add onion, garlic and curry leaves and sauté until the onion softens, about 2 minutes.

Add the fish stock, elderflower essence, rice and salt and bring to a boil on high heat. Reduce heat to low, cover and simmer until the rice is cooked and liquid absorbed, about 10 to 15 minutes.

Transfer the pilaf to a serving dish and top with the baked lobster. Serve hot.

Beetroot and Cherry Tomato Poriyal

A typical Tamil classic recipe involves sautéing the vegetable—a vibrant garnet-hued beetroot in this case—with tempered mustard seeds, onion and dressed with grated coconut. A good side dish with any meal, it doesn't take long to put together. Potatoes, peas or any seasonal vegetable works well in this recipe.

Serves 4

Ingredients

2 tablespoons coconut oil

1 teaspoon mustard seeds

4-5 curry leaves

1 red onion, finely chopped

1 green chilli, such as serrano, finely chopped

1-inch piece of ginger, finely minced

2 cloves garlic, minced

3 large beetroots, boiled, peeled and diced

Salt to taste

½ cup freshly grated coconut

8 to 10 mixed cherry tomatoes, halved

2 tablespoons coarsely chopped fresh cilantro

Directions

Heat the coconut oil in a wok over high heat. Add the mustard seeds and curry leaves and let the mustard sputter, about a minute.

Add onion, chilli, ginger and garlic and continue to cook until fragrant, about 2 to 3 minutes. Then add the beetroot and salt and stir until evenly coated with the spices. Stir in coconut, cherry tomatoes and cilantro leaves.

Serve hot.

Curry Leaf, Vodka and Sour Lime

Curry leaves and orange blossom water is a combination that surprises and pleases. At times, I add some strawberry puree to create a vibrant sour flavour.

Serves 4 to 6

Ingredients

½ cup sugar

8 to 10 curry leaves

Few drops orange blossom water

Pinch of salt

Juice of 2 lemons, or as required

Directions

In a small saucepan, combine sugar, 1 cup water, curry leaves, orange blossom water and salt over medium heat, stirring until the sugar dissolves. Remove from heat and let the flavours steep and cool to room temperature.

To serve, add sugar syrup as per taste. Squeeze in lemon juice as required and top with water or sparkling water. Serve chilled.

Fennel

Fennel

With its feathery foliage and distinct yellow flowers, fennel (*Foeniculum vulgare*) is an aromatic perennial herb from the carrot family. Originating in the Mediterranean region, it is also grown near riverbanks and coastal areas in other parts of the world.

Historically, fennel is one of the 'Nine Herbs Charm' from the 10th century Anglo-Saxon literature. The plant has a pale green bulb, from which grow feathery fine leaves with 20–50 yellow flowers blooming on short pedicels. These produce grooved fruit or seeds used as a spice. The seeds are green-brown when fresh, ideal for cooking, and greyish when dry. Wild fennel produces the most potent expensive variety in the form of small flowers known as fennel pollen.

The leaves, fruits, bulb and stalk are the edible parts of fennel with an aniseed flavour that comes from anethole. Overall, this flavour type is characterised as liquorice—fresh, slightly sweet with a touch of camphor.

The warm and pleasant fennel has been used since ancient Roman times as a vegetable and as a condiment in Indian and Chinese cooking. It is a key ingredient in the Chinese five-spice mix, garam masala and the Bengali paanch phoron. Fennel seeds are chewed as an after-meal mouth freshener and digestive, and used in desserts and drinks.

In the Mediterranean region, crunchy sweet fennel is added to pastas, seafood, salads, bread toppings and Italian sausages. The bulb is used in a variety of recipes as it can be eaten raw or cooked, grilled, sautéed, stewed or braised. The leaves are great in soups, sauces, salads and even sweet desserts, especially the young, tender ones.

India leads the production of fennel. Dried fennel seeds can be stored in airtight containers for up to two years.

Hearty Onion Soup with Fennel

Handcrafted Orange Zest Olives

Hazelnut Basil Dressing Salad

Cajun Pan Seared Trout

Creamy Spinach and Fennel Pasta

Fennel-Baked Sweet Potato Pilaf

Fennel, Cucumber and Green Chartreuse

Crispy Fennel Cookies

Hearty Onion Soup with Fennel

Onions are caramelised to a rich brown colour that forms the base for this hearty healing soup, enriched with a variety of warming spices, black pepper and sweet, earthy fennel seeds. Sometimes, I also add finely chopped seasonal vegetables.

Serves 4

Ingredients

2 tablespoons oil

3 red onions, thinly sliced

1 medium fennel bulb, trimmed and sliced

1-inch cinnamon stick

2 to 3 bay leaves

2 star anise

4 cups vegetable stock

Salt to taste

Freshly ground black pepper

1 tablespoon fennel seeds, lightly roasted and crushed

Directions

Heat oil in a heavy-bottom pan that comes with a tight-fitting lid. Add onions, sliced fennel, cinnamon, bay leaves and star anise and stir until the onions begin to caramelise around the edges, about 5 to 6 minutes.

Add stock and salt and bring to a boil on high heat. Reduce heat to low, cover and simmer until the desired consistency, about 5 to 7 minutes.

Ladle into soup bowls, garnish with crushed fennel seeds and black pepper, and serve hot.

Handcrafted Orange Zest Olives

Marinated olives are a great hors d'oeuvres, especially with cocktails. Quick and simple, the marinade combinations are endless. Here, fennel seeds and ginger powder create a tasteful flavour base for Sevillano olives, the preferred choice for marinades. I notice a lot of people generally serve store-bought olives; here I wanted to give a signature spin to these delicious bites.

Makes 1 cup

Ingredients

¼ cup extra-virgin olive oil

2 tablespoons fennel seeds

1 teaspoon dried ginger powder

Zest of ½ orange

½ teaspoon white pepper

Pinch of sugar

Salt to taste

1 cup large green brine-cured Sevillano olives, rinsed, drained and patted dry

Directions

Heat oil in a medium saucepan over medium heat. Add fennel and ginger powder and remove from heat.

Stir in the orange zest, white pepper, sugar, salt and olives and toss to coat well. Cover and let the flavours merge.

Hazelnut Basil Dressing Salad

This creamy hazelnut dressing is not only great for salads but also works well as a marinade and base for a pasta dish. Add a jalapeño if you want a little heat. Tamarind is a good substitute for vinegar.

Serves 4

Ingredients

4 tablespoons hazelnuts, lightly roasted

2 tablespoons red wine vinegar

1 cup fresh basil

2 cloves garlic

1 teaspoon salt

2 teaspoons fennel seeds

½ teaspoon black pepper

1-inch piece of galangal

¾ cup extra-virgin olive oil

3 oranges, thinly sliced

1 teaspoon honey

1 bunch rucola leaves

½ cup feta

½ cup pomegranate seeds

Directions

In a food processor, combine the hazelnuts, vinegar, basil, garlic, salt, 1 teaspoon fennel seeds, black pepper and galangal. Gradually add olive oil and process until smooth and creamy.

In a mixing bowl, toss together the sliced oranges, the remaining fennel seeds and honey.

On a salad board, arrange the salad leaves, orange slices, feta cheese and pomegranate seeds. Drizzle with the hazelnut basil dressing to serve.

Cajun Pan Seared Trout

Pan-searing fish is the best way to get crispy skin on the outside and tender flesh inside. Halibut or salmon, tuna or tilapia work equally well instead of trout. Leftovers can be made into sandwiches for lunch the next day.

Serves 4

Ingredients

3 tablespoons oil

4 tablespoons minced garlic

¼ cup orange juice

Juice and zest of 1 lime

1 teaspoon cumin powder

1 teaspoon salt

1 teaspoon finely chopped parsley

1 jalapeño, finely chopped

1 teaspoon coriander seeds, lightly crushed

4 lake trout fillets, gutted and cleaned

2 lemons, sliced in half

1 tablespoon butter

1 tablespoon fennel seeds

Radish greens for garnish

Directions

Heat 1 tablespoon oil in a skillet over medium heat. Add 3 tablespoons garlic and cook for 2 to 3 minutes. Remove from heat and transfer to a blender with orange juice, lime juice and zest, cumin, salt, parsley, jalapeño and coriander seeds. Process till smooth and creamy.

In a large mixing bowl, marinate the fish with the dressing and let it rest for 10 minutes.

In a small skillet, heat 1 tablespoon oil on medium heat. Add the remaining garlic and place lemons, cut side down, to cook for 2 to 3 minutes, until they begin to caramelise. Remove from heat and set aside.

Heat the remaining oil and butter in a heavy-bottom skillet. Add fennel seeds and stir for a minute. Sear the fish, 2 to 3 minutes on each side, until cooked through.

Garnish with radish greens and serve hot with caramelised lemons.

Creamy Spinach and Fennel Pasta

This makes for a lazy dinner, ready in a very short time. It is the cream cheese that binds the dish with subtle force. The colour and flavours of red peppers and leafy spinach in a creamy Parmesan sauce brightens the dish, with fennel adding a liquorice aftertaste.

Serves 4

Ingredients

1 cup conchiglie pasta

2 tablespoons olive oil

1 red onion, finely chopped

2 cloves garlic, minced

1 large fennel bulb, cut into thin strips

1 red pepper, cored, seeded and thinly sliced

1 celery stalk, coarsely chopped

1 spinach bunch, trimmed and roughly cut

½ cup cream cheese

¼ cup whole milk

1 teaspoon fennel seeds

Salt to taste

3 tablespoons grated Parmesan cheese

Directions

In a large stockpot, bring salted water to a boil. Add the pasta and cook, stirring occasionally until al dente. Remove from heat, drain and reserve.

Preheat the oven to 375°F.

Heat oil in a medium saucepan over medium heat. Add onion and garlic and sauté until the onion becomes soft and translucent. Add fennel, red pepper and celery and continue to cook for a couple of minutes. Add pasta, spinach, cream cheese, milk, fennel seeds and salt and stir well to combine.

Transfer to a baking dish, sprinkle with Parmesan cheese and bake until golden on top.

Serve hot.

Fennel-Baked Sweet Potato Pilaf

Whenever I make this pilaf, I never have to worry about leftovers because I can transform this dish into something different by adding grilled chicken or meats, or even stir it into a stew to make a complete meal in a bowl.

Serves 4

Ingredients

1 sweet potato, peeled and diced

2 cloves garlic, minced

Salt to taste

1 teaspoon fennel powder

Juice of 1 lemon

2 tablespoons olive oil

1 bay leaf

½-inch cinnamon stick

1 cup long-grain basmati rice

1 tablespoon fresh fennel seeds (optional)

Directions

Preheat the oven to 300°F.

In a mixing bowl, combine the sweet potatoes with garlic, salt, fennel powder, lemon juice and oil. Toss to coat well.

Place on a baking sheet in a single layer and bake for 10 to 15 minutes, until the potatoes are cooked through and crispy around the edges. Remove from the oven and set aside.

In a large pot, bring 2 cups salted water to a boil over high heat. Add rice, bay leaf and cinnamon and cook for 10 to 12 minutes, until the liquid is absorbed. Reduce heat to low, cover with a damp kitchen towel, then place the lid on top. Cook until the rice is done, about 5 to 10 minutes.

Remove from heat, add the sweet potatoes and garnish with fresh fennel seeds.

Fennel, Cucumber and Green Chartreuse

A chic cocktail with varying shades of green, this aromatic and emerald chartreuse has a distinct sweet pungency that pairs well with fresh cucumber sticks and fresh fennel seeds. Sometimes I add champagne for a sparkling taste.

Serves 4

Ingredients

4 tablespoons green chartreuse

Juice of 1 lemon, or to taste

1 tablespoon ginger juice

2 tablespoons fresh or dried fennel seeds, lightly crushed

2 tablespoons sugar syrup, or as required

1 cucumber, cut into long strips

Directions

Place ice in a pitcher, top with chartreuse, lemon juice, ginger juice, fennel seeds, water and sugar syrup. Stir well and pour into glasses over ice. Garnish with cucumber strips and serve.

Crispy Fennel Cookies

Whenever I'm cooking with children, this is one recipe I teach in the workshops. It always turns out great. Fennel seeds add a great element of surprise and texture to these cookies. The moment you taste the fennel, it changes the flavour profile on the palate.

Makes 20 to 24

Ingredients

1 cup all-purpose flour

1½ tablespoons fennel seeds

¼ cup sugar

Pinch of salt

½ cup chilled unsalted butter, cut into ½-inch cubes

Directions

Preheat the oven to 300°F.

In a mixing bowl, combine flour, fennel seeds, sugar and salt and mix well. Add unsalted butter and mix with your fingertips, until it resembles breadcrumbs.

Gather the dough and form into a ball. Wrap with plastic film and let it rest for 15 to 20 minutes.

On a lightly floured surface, roll out the dough into a square shape ¼-inch thick. Cut into 1 × 3-inch rectangles or any desired shape.

Line a baking sheet with parchment paper.

Place the dough rectangles in a single layer. Bake until golden brown and crisp, about 20 minutes.

Ginger

Ginger

Ginger (*Zingiber officinale*) originated in the tropical rainforest on the Indian subcontinent, and India is a major producer along with China, Nepal, Indonesia and Nigeria. Ginger reached Europe in the 1st century when the Romans obtained it thanks to the spice trade. Chinese philosopher Confucius is known to have included ginger in his staple diet.

Ginger is a flowering plant, a herbaceous perennial belonging to the Zingiberaceae family, which includes turmeric, cardamom and galangal plants. Growing best in warm climates, the trees bear narrow green leaves and clusters of white and pink flower buds that blossom into yellow flowers with purplish spots. The plant has underground rhizomes and the fruit is an oblong capsule enclosing smooth large seeds. The rhizome is collected when the stalk withers and sprouting is stopped via scalding, washing or scraping. This rhizome or ginger root is used as a spice as well as in medicine.

Green ginger is harvested in the sixth month of the crop, then washed to remove soil and dirt. Mature ginger is harvested in about 10 months, when the leaves dry and turn yellow; the crop is dug out carefully and the soil removed. To use fresh, they are dried for a few days and then stored. For dry ginger, the produce is soaked overnight in water, the rhizomes cleaned and the outer skin removed. They are then sun-dried for about a week, after which the rhizomes are rubbed together to remove additional skin and dirt—this is unbleached ginger. Once soaked in lime water and then dried, we get bleached ginger.

Fresh ginger is grated to obtain aromatic juice for use in cooking. Baby ginger is cream in colour and tender, free of stringy fibres and mild in flavour. Mature ginger is light tan in colour, enclosing yellow crisp flesh.

The flavour is pungent, hot and spicy with a warm rich aroma. Ginger stimulates the taste buds and makes swallowing easier. Juicy young rhizomes have a milder taste, which is great when pickled in vinegar or even cooked with other ingredients. Steeping them in water to make ginger tisane or tea, mixed with honey and lemon, is a popular practice. Young ginger has translucent skin, pink-tipped shoots and a pure fragrance. These are also used for making candy and ginger wine.

Mature rhizomes are dry and fibrous, and this root along with its juice is used as a seasoning in seafood, meat and vegetarian dishes across Asia—India, China, Korea, Japan, Vietnam, etc. In Indian cuisine, ginger along with garlic (ginger-garlic paste) is the main ingredient in curries and lentils, and in making masala chai as well as coffee. Fresh and ground ginger are both used in a six-to-one ratio, although the flavours are quite different. Ground ginger is more commonly used in baked goods like cookies and cakes, and beverages like ginger ale and ginger beer.

Candied or crystallised ginger is made by cooking the root in sugar until it is soft.

Fresh ginger leaves are used in Vietnamese soups, while in Japan, the flower buds are eaten. The wild ginger flower is used in Thailand and Malaysia. In Thai cooking, galangal is similar to ginger; it belongs to the ginger family and is called Thai ginger. In the Caribbean drink sorrel, ginger is an integral spice. In the West, ginger is used in cookies, schnapps and liqueur.

Ginger is also valued for its medicinal properties; dry ginger is found in oils, essences and soft drinks.

Fresh ginger rhizomes are hard, plump with relatively wrinkle free skin, and keep well in the refrigerator for up to 10 days, or sealed in the freezer for up to three months. Ginger is also available as chopped or as a paste as well.

Bamboo Shoot and Ginger Chicken Soup

Braised Red Cabbage, Apple and Raw
Mango Salad

Warm Carrot and Cranberry Medley in
Sage-Cardamom Butter

Coconut Simmered Pan-Roasted Chicken

Ricotta-Stuffed Baked Cauliflower

Soba Noodles with Star Anise-Infused Oil

Homemade Gingerade

Satiny Ginger Chocolate Ice Cream

Bamboo Shoot and Ginger Chicken Soup

There is nothing more comforting than a bowl of hot soup, especially one that is filled with the warmth of ginger, crunchy bamboo shoots and the sublime flavour of chicken. This soup is always a crowd-pleaser—a one-pot wonder.

Many times, I fry a batch of noodles and store them in an airtight container and use it to garnish my soups and sometimes even rice dishes.

Serves 4 to 6

Ingredients

Vegetable oil for frying

4 to 6 ounces egg noodles

16 ounces finely chopped chicken breast

1 tablespoon soy sauce

3-inch piece of ginger, peeled and minced

2 to 3 cloves garlic, minced

Juice of 1 lemon

5 cups chicken stock

1 bamboo shoot, peeled and finely chopped

6 to 8 button mushrooms, finely chopped

1 tablespoon tomato puree

1 tablespoon hot sauce, or to taste

Salt to taste

2 tablespoons corn starch mixed with
4 tablespoons water

Directions

Heat the oil in a wok over high heat to 350°F. Add the noodles and fry till golden brown. Remove with a slotted spoon and drain on a paper towel. Reserve for garnish.

In a mixing bowl, combine the chicken with soy sauce, ginger, garlic and lemon juice and set aside for at least 10 to 15 minutes.

In a medium saucepan over high heat, bring the stock to a boil. Reduce the heat to medium and add the chicken, bamboo shoots, mushrooms, tomato puree, hot sauce and salt, and cook until the chicken is cooked and the flavours are well combined, about 3 to 4 minutes. Add the corn starch mixture and stir continuously until the soup is thick and creamy, or the required consistency is reached.

Garnish with crispy noodles and serve hot.

Braised Red Cabbage, Apple and Raw Mango Salad

The richness and crispy texture of this simple salad is a great addition to any meal. Garnishing with toasted nuts adds to its heartiness and makes it more satisfying and filling.

Serves 4

Ingredients

2 ounces bacon, cut into ½-inch pieces

2-inch piece of ginger, minced

2 cloves garlic, crushed

1 red cabbage head, halved, cored and coarsely shredded

2 tablespoons red wine vinegar

1 teaspoon sugar

Salt to taste

Freshly ground black pepper

1 green mango, pitted and cut into strips

1 red apple, cored and cut into strips

Microgreens for garnish

Directions

In a large heavy-bottom pan over medium heat, cook the bacon, stirring occasionally until it becomes fragrant, crisp and the fat renders, about 6 to 8 minutes.

Add the ginger and garlic and cook for a minute. Then add the cabbage, vinegar, sugar, salt and black pepper and continue to cook for about 2 minutes.

Add the mango and apple and toss to combine the flavours.

Garnish with microgreens and serve.

Warm Carrot and Cranberry Medley in Sage-Cardamom Butter

During fall, when carrots are in season, this quick and easy recipe makes its way to tables, sometimes as a side dish and even as a main. Carrot and cranberry are glazed in warm sage and cardamom-flavoured butter along with spicy and tart notes from ginger and lemon juice, with roasted cashews adding a nice crunch.

Serves 4

Ingredients

3 tablespoons unsalted butter

3 to 4 cardamom pods

Ginger juice

10 to 12 sage leaves

10 to 12 carrots, cut into sticks

¼ cup cranberries

Salt to taste

½ cup vegetable stock, or as required

Juice of 1 lime

3 tablespoons ginger juice

8 to 10 cashews, lightly roasted

Chives for garnish

Directions

Melt the butter in a medium skillet over medium-high heat. Add cardamom, ginger juice and sage and cook until fragrant. The leaves should curl around the edges and the butter a dark amber (but not burnt), about 4 to 5 minutes.

Remove the sage and cardamom and add the carrots, cranberries and salt. Stir to coat evenly. Add the vegetable stock and continue to cook until the carrots are cooked and the mixture is dry. Stir in lime and ginger juices and toss to coat evenly.

Garnish with cashews and chives and serve.

Coconut Simmered Pan-Roasted Chicken

The pan-roasted flavours of chicken cooked with coconut and lemon juice are sublime and fragrant. At times I also add kaffir lime leaves or Thai basil while simmering the chicken in coconut milk. You can increase the quantity of coconut milk if you prefer.

Serves 4 to 6

Ingredients

2 cups coconut milk

3-inch piece of ginger, minced

3 to 4 cloves garlic, chopped

1 green chilli, such as serrano, minced

2 tablespoons olive oil

Juice of 1 lemon, plus more for garnish

Salt to taste

Freshly ground black pepper

2½ pounds chicken legs

1 tablespoon oyster sauce

1 tablespoon soy sauce

1 tablespoon tomato paste

Directions

In a mixing bowl, combine the coconut milk, ginger, garlic, green chilli, oil, lemon juice, salt, pepper and chicken legs and toss to coat evenly. Cover and marinate in a refrigerator for 3 to 4 hours, preferably overnight.

Transfer the chicken to a medium saucepan and cook on low heat. Add oyster sauce, soy sauce and tomato paste and cook until the mixture begins to dry and the chicken is cooked through.

Serve hot with a side of vegetables and lemon.

Ricotta-Stuffed Baked Cauliflower

Baking cauliflower takes it to a whole new level with just a few simple flavourings like Madras curry powder, which is available in speciality stores, in different heat levels—mild, medium, hot. Choose depending on your preference. Ricotta cheese is a great, versatile ingredient for adding a creamy lightness to dishes.

Serves 4

Ingredients

½ cup ricotta cheese

1 teaspoon cumin seeds

1 teaspoon coriander seeds, lightly crushed

¼ cup candied ginger, finely chopped

Salt to taste

1 cauliflower head, cut into florets

3 tablespoons olive oil, plus more for greasing

1 tablespoon Madras curry powder

1 medium-size red pepper, cored and diced

Juice of 1 lemon, or to taste

2-inch piece of ginger, julienned

Fresh cilantro for garnish

Directions

Preheat the oven to 375°F.

In a mixing bowl, combine ricotta, cumin, coriander, candied ginger and salt. Gently stuff the cauliflower florets with the ricotta mixture.

In a large mixing bowl, combine oil, Madras curry powder, red pepper, lemon juice and ginger juliennes. Add the stuffed cauliflower to this mixture and gently toss to coat evenly.

On a lightly greased baking tray, place the cauliflower in a single layer and bake for 15 to 20 minutes, until it's tender and cooked.

Garnish with cilantro and serve hot.

Soba Noodles with Star Anise-Infused Oil

Warm and filling, gluten-free nutty buckwheat soba noodles with wholesome vegetables is a perfect meal in a bowl. You can make this infused oil in larger quantities with your choice of spices and flavourings, and store.

Serves 4

Ingredients

½ pound soba noodles

4 tablespoons sesame oil

2 star anise

1 teaspoon black peppercorns

2-inch cinnamon stick

2 dried red chillies

2-inch piece of ginger, minced

1 small green zucchini, thinly sliced

1 small yellow zucchini, thinly sliced

1 teaspoon orange zest

1 tablespoon fish sauce

1 tablespoon soy sauce

Salt to taste

Chives for garnish

Directions

Bring salted water to a boil in a stockpot over high heat. Add the soba noodles and cook until al dente. Drain and set aside.

Heat sesame oil in a small saucepan over high heat. Remove from heat and add star anise, peppercorns, cinnamon and red chillies. Cover and let all the flavours infuse.

In a medium wok, heat 2 tablespoons of infused sesame oil on medium-high heat. Stir-fry ginger and zucchini. Add the noodles and orange zest, fish sauce, soy sauce and cook until the flavours merge and the noodles are well coated.

Season with salt and garnish with chives. Drizzle with the remaining infused oil and serve hot.

Homemade Gingerade

Floral, savoury and spicy notes of ginger make this homemade drink delicious and comforting whether served hot or chilled. It can be a great start to an evening of entertainment. The syrup can be made ahead of time and stored in a sterilised airtight container in the refrigerator for up to 3 weeks.

Serves 4 to 6

Ingredients

1 cup sugar

¾ cup finely chopped ginger

2 tablespoons fennel seeds

2-inch cinnamon stick

Juice of 3 lemons

Mint springs for garnish

Directions

In a medium stockpot, add sugar and lightly caramelise on low heat, till it turns fragrant and golden brown. Add ginger, fennel, cinnamon and 8 cups of water.

Increase the heat to high and bring to a boil. Reduce heat to low, cover and simmer for 4 to 5 minutes, until very fragrant. Remove from heat and let it stand covered to allow the flavours steep. Cool to room temperature then stir in the lemon juice.

Strain, pour over ice and top with water, seltzer or champagne. Garnish with mint and serve.

Satiny Ginger Chocolate Ice Cream

A deep rich chocolate ice cream is an all-time delight. Ginger adds just the right amount of spice that enhances the ice cream experience. Candied ginger not only adds texture but also a nice sugary touch. You can also top with nuts of your choice.

Serves 4

Ingredients

8 egg yolks

1 cup brown sugar

6 ounces bittersweet chocolate, melted

2 tablespoons unsweetened cocoa powder

1 ½ tablespoons dried ginger powder

2 cups milk

2 cups heavy cream

¼ cup coarsely chopped candied ginger

Directions

In a medium saucepan, combine egg yolk, sugar, chocolate, cocoa powder and ginger powder. Whisk continuously until well blended.

Cook over medium heat and gently add milk, whisking until the mixture begins to thicken and evenly coats the back of a spoon, about 8 to 10 minutes.

Strain into a mixing bowl using a fine mesh strainer. Add the cream and candied ginger and let it cool to room temperature.

Process in an ice-cream maker according to the manufacturer's instructions until the ice cream is creamy and fluffy.

Transfer to an airtight plastic container and freeze until set.

Kokum

Kokum

Kokum (*Garcinia indica*), native to India's western coastline, is a fruit-bearing tree of the mangosteen family. Though popular in the Indian subcontinent, its recognition in the global market is limited.

Also known as the kokum butter tree, the fruit has been an integral part of India's history and culture. The fruit, leaves, seeds, oil and bark are valued for its culinary and medicinal/Ayurvedic properties as well as a superfood filled with antioxidants and antibacterial powers.

This tropical evergreen tree reaches a height of approximately 50 feet, with a dense canopy-like foliage. The young leaves are tender and tinted with red, while the mature leaves are dark green glossy, lance-like and oblong. The tree produces dark pink flowers from November to February, which grow mostly in clusters.

The berry-like spherical fruit is red and purple, which turns brown-red and blackish red when ripe, with a sweet aroma. The darker the fruit, the better it is regarded. Filled with five to eight large seeds, these are 60 per cent kernel and 40 per cent oil. The fruit is collected manually in April and May, when the branches are shaken with sticks and the fruit falls. The rind of the fruit is soaked in the pulpy juice, sun-dried, then made available as a spice folded into leathery strips. The fruit is then split or broken to obtain the seeds, which are pressed into the pulp. Kokum oil or butter is a light grey-yellow, melts on contact with skin and is a good substitute for cocoa butter.

Kokum is used as a souring agent especially along the west coast, in the cuisines of Goa, Karnataka and Maharashtra (Konkan region) as well as Kerala and Gujarat. The dry sticky rind, dark purple or black in colour, lends a pinkish-purple hue to food and an astringent, sweet-sour flavour with a fruity, balsamic aroma. Malic and tartaric acids contribute to the sour taste of kokum. The dried outer covering is used as a spice known as aamsul.

Kokum is a substitute for tamarind in curries, especially those that include coconut, potatoes and lentils. It is also a good seasoning for fish curries, where it is added whole and not chopped, as well as in chutneys and pickles. When used whole, kokum needs to be removed before eating as the seeds are large and hard. Dry kokum is soaked in water for a while, then the soft pulp is pressed dry and the liquid used in cooking. Since kokum is strong, too much can lead to overpowering sourness and saltiness, so seasoning needs to be checked accordingly. A popular preparation is Sol Kadhi where kokum is mixed with coconut milk.

Kokum is readily available in local markets when in season and abundantly grown in courtyards of homes in the region it is indigenous to. Besides dried rind and paste, the fruit preserved in sugar makes for a bright red syrup that's mixed into a cooling healthy cordial, especially in summer. The kokum seed is used in medicines, cosmetics and confectionery too, while kokum oil is added to cosmetics, soaps and lotions because of its stable oxidative and emollient properties.

Coconut and Kokum Welcome Drink

Green Mango and Lamb Salad

Dried Shrimp Stir-Fry with Kokum

Mrs Pacheco's Fish Curry

Pan-Fried Crispy Eggplant

Bartlett Pear and Corn Pulao

Kokum Sandalwood Cooler

Coconut and Kokum Welcome Drink

A great start to a meal, this is a traditional drink from the coastal region of India. Sour kokum and sweet coconut combine with green chillies, making it not just a welcome drink but also an appetite enhancer. Roasted cumin is an excellent garnish.

Serves 4 to 6

Ingredients

1 cup dried kokum petals

3 cups coconut milk

2 tablespoons coconut oil

2 teaspoons mustard seeds

8 to 10 fresh curry leaves

1-inch piece of ginger, minced

1 teaspoon sugar

1 green chilli, such as serrano, seeded and split

Salt to taste

Directions

In a stockpot, combine kokum petals with ¼ cup water and bring to a light simmer over medium heat. Add the coconut milk and bring to a boil. Remove from heat, cautiously transfer to a food processor and process to a smooth mixture. Strain if required.

Heat oil in a pan over medium heat. Add the mustard seeds, let them sputter (about 30 seconds), then stir in the curry leaves and ginger. Cook for about a minute, until fragrant. Add the kokum mixture, sugar and green chilli and simmer for a minute, until the flavours are well combined. Season with salt and serve warm.

Green Mango and Lamb Salad

This warm, comforting salad is a great quick meal to make. Even though they have distinct taste profiles, you can use tamarind pulp instead of kokum. Papaya or other tropical fruits are a good substitute for green mango.

Leftovers make a good filling for wraps.

Serves 4 to 6

Ingredients

2 pounds boneless leg of lamb, trimmed of fat and cut into 2-inch pieces

Salt to taste

1 teaspoon turmeric

½ teaspoon freshly ground black pepper

1 teaspoon chilli powder

3 tablespoons vegetable oil

2 tablespoons kokum paste

2 cloves garlic, minced

1 medium red onion, thinly sliced

2 medium firm tomatoes, sliced

1 green mango, peeled, pitted and cut into strips

Fresh cilantro for garnish

Juice of 1 lemon, or to taste

2 tablespoons extra-virgin olive oil

Directions

In a mixing bowl, season the lamb with salt and turmeric and let it rest for 10 minutes at room temperature.

In a small mixing bowl, combine pepper, chilli powder, 1 tablespoon oil, kokum and garlic and whisk. Pour this mixture over the lamb and toss to evenly coat.

In a heavy cast-iron skillet, heat the remaining oil over medium heat. Add the seasoned lamb strips and cook until golden brown. Remove from heat and transfer to a mixing bowl.

Add onion, tomatoes, green mangoes and cilantro. Squeeze in lemon juice, add salt and olive oil and toss to coat well. Serve warm.

Dried Shrimp Stir-Fry with Kokum

This easy recipe with crispy and garlicky shrimp and green mango highlights the tanginess of kokum. A few dried kokum petals can add a strong sour flavour and should be used sparingly.

Serves 4

Ingredients

2 tablespoons peanut oil

2 cloves garlic, minced

3 shallots, minced

1 green chilli, such as serrano, chopped

2 cups dried shrimp

Salt to taste

2 tender green mangoes, pitted and sliced

4 to 6 kokum petals

1 medium tomato, chopped

Directions

In a skillet, heat oil over medium heat. Add garlic, shallots and chilli and stir for a minute, until fragrant.

Add the dried shrimps and a pinch of salt, then put in green mango, kokum petals and tomatoes, and stir well.

Serve hot.

Mrs Pacheco's Fish Curry

Indian home cooking is very inspiring and robust with minimum use of ingredients. Though tomato paste is my addition to the recipe, the dish works well even without it. The highlight of this dish is the freshly ground coconut mixture—truly worth trying.

Serves 4

Ingredients

2 medium pomfret, scaled, gilled and gutted

½ teaspoon salt, plus more to taste

1 teaspoon turmeric

1 cup grated coconut

3 dried red chillies, coarsely chopped and soaked in 2 tablespoons warm water

1 teaspoon coriander seeds, lightly crushed

2 cloves garlic, minced

1-inch piece of ginger, peeled and coarsely chopped

1 green chilli, such as serrano, slit and coarsely chopped

2 tablespoons oil

2 tablespoons tomato paste

1 cup fish stock

4 to 6 kokum petals

2 small potatoes, peeled and boiled

Directions

In a mixing bowl, evenly rub the fish with salt and turmeric. Let it rest for 10 minutes at room temperature.

In a food processor, combine coconut, soaked red chillies, coriander, garlic, ginger and green chilli, and process to a smooth paste, adding a little water if required.

Heat oil in a medium saucepan over medium heat. Add coconut mixture, tomato paste, fish stock, kokum and salt and bring to a boil. Add the fish and potatoes and simmer, covered, until cooked through, about 8 to 10 minutes. Gently turn the fish if required.

Serve hot with boiled rice.

Pan-Fried Crispy Eggplant

Different versions of fried eggplant can be found in cuisines across cultures around the world. This simple recipe can be made in a very short time and is a real crowd-pleaser. You can use a wire rack and bake in the oven for a healthier version or even serve over a sauce as an entrée.

Serves 4

Ingredients

1 medium eggplant,
cut into ½ to ⅓-inch thick slices

2 tablespoons kokum paste

1 teaspoon turmeric

½ teaspoon salt

⅓ cup all-purpose flour

⅓ cup rice flour

1 teaspoon red chilli powder

1 teaspoon cumin powder

4 tablespoons vegetable oil, or as required

Directions

In a mixing bowl, marinate the eggplant with kokum paste, turmeric and salt and set aside for 5 minutes at room temperature.

In another bowl, sift together the flours, chilli powder and cumin. Transfer the mixture to a plate and make a single layer.

Heat the oil in a heavy-bottom skillet over medium heat. Dredge the eggplant slices in the flour mixture and sear in the hot oil until crisp and golden brown, about 2 minutes on each side. Remove with a slotted spoon and drain on kitchen towels. Serve hot and fresh.

Bartlett Pear and Corn Pulao

There are so many variations of the pear-and-kokum combination, which work well in a range of dishes from meat stews to desserts and rice pilafs. This recipe also lends itself to mangoes and peaches. You can add a hint of spice with green chilli or cayenne pepper, as per your taste.

Serves 4

Ingredients

2 tablespoons vegetable oil

3 shallots, minced

1 cup long-grain basmati rice, washed, rinsed, soaked in water for 10 minutes and drained

1 bay leaf

Salt to taste

2 cups vegetable stock

4 kokum petals, soaked in ¼ cup warm water for 10 minutes and drained

½ cup corn kernels

1 ripe pear, such as Bartlett, finely chopped

Juice of 1 lemon

Directions

In a saucepan, heat oil over medium heat. Add shallots and cook until translucent, 2 to 3 minutes. Add rice, bay leaf, salt and vegetable stock. Bring to a boil over high heat and cook until the water is absorbed.

Reduce heat to low and stir in kokum, corn, pear and lemon juice. Cover rice with a damp cloth and a tight-fitting lid, and cook for about 5 more minutes.

Serve hot.

Kokum Sandalwood Cooler

Sometimes, the addition of a simple ingredient can make a drink more memorable. In this, it is the aroma of sandalwood, which elevates the flavours. Ginger juice adds the required touch of warm spiciness needed to balance the taste.

Serves 6

Ingredients

1 cup dried kokum petals

½ cup sugar

2 tablespoons ginger juice

1 teaspoon sandalwood essence

Mint leaves for garnish

Directions

In a stockpot, add kokum petals, sugar, ginger juice, sandalwood essence and 2 cups of water and bring to a boil over high heat. Remove from heat, cautiously transfer to a food processor and process to a smooth mixture. Strain into a pitcher and refrigerate to chill.

To serve, pour over ice, top with water and garnish with mint leaves.

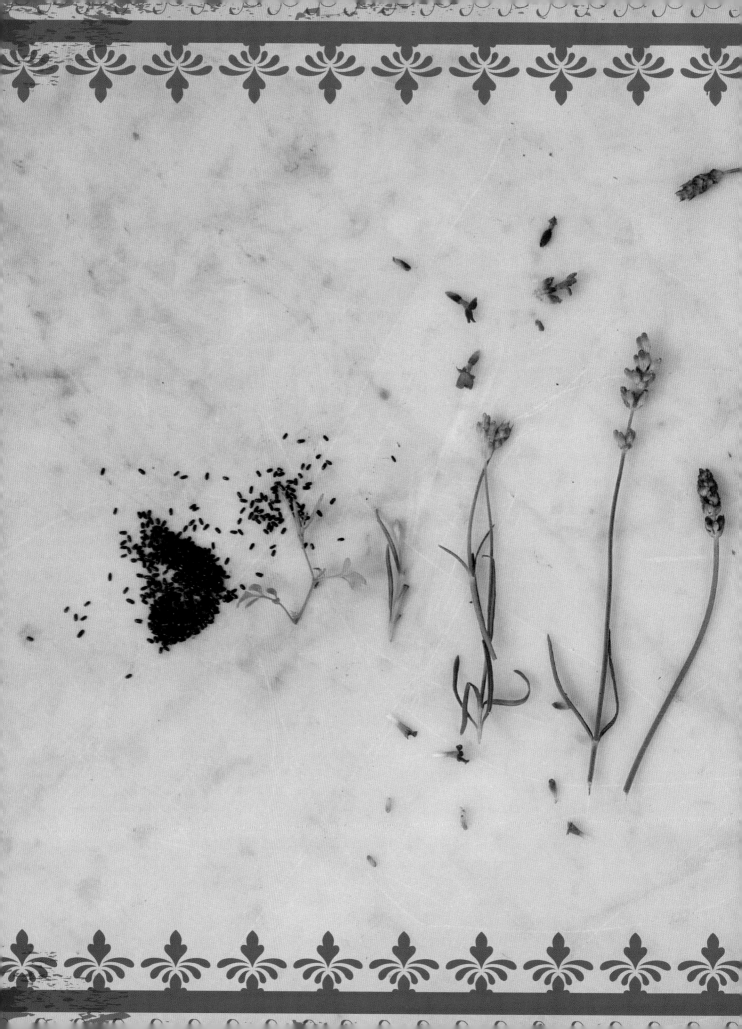

Lavender

Lavender

Lavender (*Lavandula angustifolia*) belongs to the mint family of flowering plants or Lamiaceae. Native to the Mediterranean region, Europe, northern and eastern Africa, southeast India and southwest Asia, it is cultivated as a culinary herb, for its essential oils and as a decoration plant as well as.

The colour lavender gets its name from the particular shade of the flowers. The level of camphor content in the plant determines which lavender is better to use in cooking. Low camphor English lavender—is the best lavender to cook with then the French lavender or Spanish lavender, which has a strong camphor content. Historically considered a holy herb, it was used to prepare a holy essence in the Song of Songs book of the Bible.

Growing well in temperate climate, the lavender's leaves vary in shape from simple to pinnate. Blue, lilac, violet, yellowish and black flowers grow in whorls, rising above the leaf foliage on spikes. In full bloom, fields are a beautiful purple sight to behold. The region of Provence is filled with the colour and fragrance of lavender because of the abundance of fields around Luberon in southern France. They bloom from the last week of June, peak in early July and are harvested in August. The flowers are harvested before they completely open—this is when their oil is most potent.

The harvest season also depends upon end use. For fresh or dried flowers, this happens when the one or two blooms appear, because collecting lavender once the flowers have already bloomed will end in most flowers and buds falling off the stems when tied. If harvesting buds, the correct time is when up to half of the flowers have bloomed in the field. For oil, the correct time is when half the flowers have withered so that maximum quantity and highest quality can be obtained.

Lavender is gathered and tied in small bundles together. It is dried immediately after harvest to get the best colour and quality. This is generally done by hanging small bundles upside down with a paper clip on a wire or hook in a dark space with good ventilation. If the buds are to be used, they are collected immediately after drying and packed in sealed containers.

Lavender adds a sweet, floral flavour with lemony notes when used. Since it is concentrated and potent, a little bit is enough. Dried flowers can be mixed with sugar or simply ground with sugar to make lavender sugar, which is great for baked goods. Mostly, the dried buds are used in cooking as they contain the oil, aroma and taste.

Fresh flowers can be added before baking, put into compotes and preserves, and used to infuse sorbets, milk and syrups. Lavender pairs well with savoury items too and in salads, roasts, marinades and rubs. Herb mixtures with lavender are popular in Mediterranean cooking, and also in Morocco. Honey is obtained from the nectar of the flowers. Candied flowers and flavoured sugar are good decorations for cakes, while baked goods use lavender essence as it pairs well with chocolate.

Originally, southern France was the centre of lavender distillation, but now essential oil is also produced in Bulgaria, Russia, Australia and other Mediterranean countries. Lavender oil, besides being valued for aromatherapy, has anti-inflammatory and antiseptic properties and is used in balms and salves. With chamomile, it is very helpful for aromatherapy, anxiety reduction and addressing other disorders.

The pale purple flowers also find their way into potpourris, dry flower arrangements, linen fresheners and fragrant water.

Gailon Broccoli and Labneh Soup

Purple Asparagus with Lavender Salt

Chioggia Beet with Passion Fruit and
Lavender Vinaigrette

Lavender Butter-Tossed Romanesco with
Blood Orange Segments

Lavender Honey Roast Chicken

Red Quinoa with Orange Habanero

Blackberry and Lavender Jam Tarts

Lavender and Pineberry Cooler

Gailon Broccoli and Labneh Soup

I always buy culinary lavender for cooking, which is suitable for consumption. It adds a wonderful floral surprise to each spoonful of this soup. You can use hung yogurt or Greek yogurt for this recipe instead of labneh, which harmonises the delicate flavour of lavender.

Serves 4

Ingredients

2 tablespoons vegetable oil

1 medium red onion, finely chopped

2 cloves garlic, minced

1 bay leaf

1 cup chopped gailon broccoli

2 cups vegetable stock

Salt to taste

¼ teaspoon lavender buds, finely crushed

2 cups labneh or Greek yogurt

½ teaspoon cinnamon

1 teaspoon chilli powder

Directions

Heat oil in a saucepan over medium heat. Add onion, garlic and bay leaf and cook until the onion is translucent, about 3 to 4 minutes. Add the broccoli and toss well.

Reserve some of the onion-broccoli mix for garnish.

Add vegetable stock to the remaining mixture, along with salt and crushed lavender and bring to a boil over high heat. Remove from heat and stir in labneh.

Ladle the soup into bowls. Mix cinnamon and chilli powder and sprinkle over the soup. Top with the reserved garnish and serve hot.

Purple Asparagus with Lavender Salt

Though similar but slightly sweeter than the white and green varieties, purple asparagus elevates the dish with its beautiful violet hues. Serve with lemon wedges to add a citrusy undertone alongside the delicately flavoured lavender salt.

Serves 4

Ingredients

For lavender salt

6 tablespoons sea salt

2 tablespoons cumin powder

1 teaspoon ground lemon rind

1 teaspoon lavender buds, finely ground

1 tablespoon olive oil

3 cloves garlic, minced

Juice of 1 lemon

1 teaspoon cayenne pepper

2 pounds fresh purple asparagus, trimmed

White pepper to taste

Directions

In a sterilised clean jar, combine salt, cumin powder, lemon rind powder and lavender.

Shake to mix well and store tightly covered at room temperature for 2 to 3 days before using.

In a mixing bowl, combine oil, garlic, lemon juice and cayenne pepper, and toss the asparagus to coat evenly.

Heat a grilling pan over medium heat and lightly grease it. Add the asparagus and cook until the asparagus is lightly charred.

Arrange on a serving platter and sprinkle with white pepper and lavender salt.

Chioggia Beet with Passion Fruit and Lavender Vinaigrette

The watercolour painting-like appearance of Chioggia beets shines in this simple recipe. I prefer to serve them raw with a simple flavourful vinaigrette to preserve their crunch and beauty. I like to use fresh passion fruit pulp along with seeds for a great texture, but you can also use passion fruit puree.

Serves 4

Ingredients

1 small shallot, minced

2 cloves garlic, minced

1 teaspoon lavender extract

2 tablespoons red wine vinegar

4 tablespoons passion fruit puree or pulp

2 teaspoons Dijon mustard

¾ cup extra-virgin olive oil

Salt to taste

Freshly ground black pepper

4 to 6 Chioggia beets

Fresh mint for garnish

Directions

In a mixing bowl, add shallot, garlic, lavender extract, vinegar, passion fruit puree and Dijon mustard and whisk to combine. Slowly drizzle olive oil and continuously whisk until emulsified. Season with salt and pepper.

Place beets in a salad bowl and drizzle with the vinaigrette. Toss gently to coat the beets well. Garnish with mint leaves and serve immediately.

Lavender Butter-Tossed Romanesco with Blood Orange Segments

For me, Romanesco is the crown jewel among vegetables. While cooking, I always want to enhance and display its beauty rather than submerging it in sauces. Its sweetness is great for salads and roasting.

Serves 4

Ingredients

1 Romanesco head, trimmed and cut into florets

2 tablespoons unsalted butter

1-inch piece of ginger, minced

Juice of 1 lemon

12 teaspoons lavender buds, lightly crushed

6 garlic cloves, browned and crushed

Salt to taste

Freshly ground white pepper

Fresh dill for garnish

Directions

Bring salted water to a boil in a stockpot over high heat. Add the Romanesco florets for 1 to 2 minutes. Remove from heat and set aside.

Heat the butter in a saucepan over medium heat. Stir in the ginger, lemon juice, lavender and garlic and cook for a minute until the flavours are well combined. Add the Romanesco and toss gently to coat well. Season with salt and pepper.

Place on a serving platter, garnish with dill and serve with blood orange segments.

Lavender Honey Roast Chicken

For me, this chicken dish is the true flavour of Provence, where the lavender fields inspire the cuisine of the area. No festive occasion is complete without a roast chicken in the centre of the table. If you need to stuff the chicken, you can use pulao rice with nuts, vegetables or even minced chicken.

Serves 4

Ingredients

One 6-pound chicken, skin and giblets removed

1 medium onion, diced

8 to 10 garlic cloves

1 cup chicken broth

1 teaspoon salt

For the marinade

1 teaspoon sweet paprika

½ teaspoon cinnamon powder

1 tablespoon onion powder

1 teaspoon garlic powder

½ teaspoon lavender bud powder

Salt to taste

Freshly ground black pepper

½ teaspoon brown sugar

1 teaspoon all-purpose flour

1 lemon, zested and juiced

3 tablespoons olive oil

1 tablespoon honey

2 tablespoons oil

Directions

Preheat the oven to 425°F.

Rinse the chicken inside and out under cold running water, then dry thoroughly using paper towels. Rub salt and let it rest for 15 to 20 minutes.

In a mixing bowl, combine all the marinade ingredients and rub evenly on the chicken.

In a heavy-bottom oven-proof skillet, heat the oil over medium heat. Add the onion, garlic and chicken, and gently sear until evenly browned on all sides.

Remove from heat and pour the broth into the skillet. Place in the oven until the chicken is cooked through, about 25 to 30 minutes.

Remove from oven and let the chicken rest for about 10 minutes before carving.

Serve with rice or flatbread.

Red Quinoa with Orange Habanero

Habanero is a popular Mexican chilli, and a little goes a long way due to its hotness levels. Quinoa is not a grain but the seed of a grain-like crop related to beets. It is very necessary to rinse the quinoa thoroughly using a fine mesh strainer to remove the bitterness.

Serves 4

Ingredients

1 tablespoon salt, plus more to taste

1 lavender sprig

1 cup red quinoa, thoroughly rinsed

2 tablespoons finely chopped red pepper

2 tablespoons coarsely chopped fresh mint

2 small shallots, coarsely chopped

2 tablespoons extra-virgin olive oil

½ teaspoon honey

1 fresh orange habanero, coarsely chopped

Directions

Bring 4 cups of water with salt and lavender sprig to a boil in a stockpot over high heat. Add quinoa and continue to boil until the quinoa opens up, about 15 to 20 minutes.

Discard the lavender, strain the quinoa and set aside.

In a mixing bowl, combine red pepper, mint, shallots, olive oil, honey, orange habanero and salt. Toss in quinoa and mix well.

Serve immediately.

Blackberry and Lavender Jam Tarts

Though these tarts appear difficult and complicated to make, I have tried to simplify the process so that everyone can whip up this wonderful festive delight at home. You can use any fruit of your choice; just ensure the mixture is not too wet. Once you get the hang of the lattice and filling, you'll have greater creative freedom.

Makes 3 tarts

Ingredients

1¼ cups plain flour, plus more for dusting

6 tablespoons cold unsalted butter, cut into cubes

¼ teaspoon salt

2 cups fresh blackberries

1 teaspoon dried ginger powder

½ teaspoon orange zest

½ teaspoon lavender extract

1 tablespoon fresh lemon juice

1 egg white, whisked with 2 tablespoons milk

Directions

Preheat the oven to 375°F.

To make the dough, mix the flour, butter and salt in a bowl with your fingertips until the mixture resembles coarse crumbs. Add 2 tablespoons iced water, and more if necessary, to form a firm dough. Pat into a disc, dust lightly with flour and wrap in cling film. Place in the refrigerator to chill for at least 1 hour.

On a lightly floured surface, roll out the dough to make three 4-inch circles. Reserve the remaining dough for the lattice.

Gently ease the dough into three 3-inch tart tins with removable bottoms. Prick the dough all over with a fork and chill in the refrigerator for at least 30 minutes.

Line the pastry with greaseproof paper and fill with pie weights or baking beans. Bake until the pastry begins to colour around the edges, 8 to 10 minutes. Remove the paper and weights and continue to bake just until the pastry dries out and turns light golden, about 4 to 8 minutes longer. Cool completely on a wire rack before filling.

In a medium saucepan, combine blackberries, ginger, orange zest, lavender extract and lemon juice and cook over medium-low heat until the mixture comes together in a jam-like consistency.

Fill the tart shells with the blackberry mixture. Top with dough strips in desired pattern and brush with the egg wash.

Bake for 20 to 25 minutes, until golden.

Remove from the oven and cool on a wire rack. Serve with any ice cream of your choice.

Lavender and Pineberry Cooler

This lavender sugar syrup is great in a variety of recipes from drinks to desserts. The subtle floral aroma and flavours of lemon, ginger and lavender are very addictive. Though pineberries look like strawberries, they have a wonderful pineapple-like flavour, white colouring and red seeds. You can use seasonal berries if you like.

This drink also tastes equally good served warm.

Serves 6 to 8

Ingredients

1 cup sugar

Juice of 2 lemons

2 tablespoons ginger juice

12 to 15 lavender sprigs

15 to 20 pineberries

Directions

Combine the sugar, ½ cup water, lemon and ginger juices and lavender sprigs in a saucepan and bring to a boil over medium heat, stirring constantly until the sugar has dissolved. Remove from heat, cool to room temperature and chill.

To serve, pour the syrup over ice, top with water or seltzer and garnish with pineberries.

Mango Powder

Also *Mangifera indica*, this citrusy fruity seasoning is made by sun-drying peeled and thinly sliced raw mangoes to a woody colour and texture. The dried strips are available whole or ground as a fine beige powder known as amchoor in Hindi. Produced in India only, the first crop of mangoes is harvested for best flavour.

The mango tree is distinct in its massive size and deep-green leaves. Its bark, leaves, flowers, seeds and fruit, all are edible, while its acidity comes from citric acid.

The fragrance and tartness lend acidity and a mango flavour to dishes ranging from soups to curries, chutneys and snacks. Raw mango powder is also used in marinades for fish, meats and poultry, as well as a topping. It adds sourness without moisture, and the tropical flavour is an important part of the spice mix chaat masala used in fruit salads and sprinkled on snacks.

Amchoor is used as a substitute for tamarind in south India and an alternative for lemon juice. When using dried mango strips in curries, remove before serving. The dried mango is also used in pickles and in north Indian food, especially recipes from Punjab region. Available in speciality markets, the dried slices keep well for up to four months. The powder can be stored for a year in an airtight container.

Noodle and Vegetable Broth with Yuzu

Crabmeat Croquette Salad

Family Favourite Peach Frittata

Green Mango and Shrimp Curry

Crispy Okra with Mango Powder Spice Mix

Vetiver and Green Mango Shrub

Strawberry and Vanilla Cream
with Meringue

Noodle and Vegetable Broth with Yuzu

Yuzu from Japan is truly a blessing in our kitchens. The tangy and tart pulp is used in recipes to impart a different sourness than lemons. A good substitute for it would be a combination of lemon, lime juice and rinds. Since any amalgamation of ingredients can be used in this broth soup, it is a great recipe for last-minute dinners using available ingredients.

Serves 4 to 6

Ingredients

1 tablespoon sesame oil

2 cloves garlic, minced

4 to 5 dried red chillies

4 to 6 ounces egg noodles

6 cups vegetable stock

½ cup baby corn

½ cup mushrooms, diced

½ cup zucchini, sliced

½ cup red cabbage

½ cup beans, sliced

2 teaspoons dried mango powder

1 tablespoon light soy sauce

1 tablespoon yuzu syrup

Salt to taste

Directions

Heat oil in a wok over medium heat. Add garlic and red chillies and sauté for about a minute.

Add noodles and vegetable stock and cook until the noodles are half-done, about 2 to 3 minutes. Put in vegetables and stir well.

Season with mango powder, soy sauce, yuzu syrup and salt. Continue to cook until the noodles are done and the vegetables crunchy, about 2 to 3 minutes.

Ladle into bowls and serve.

Crabmeat Croquette Salad

Whenever I'm unsure about the menu for dinner parties, this recipe is a lifesaver as it stands for two courses—salad and appetiser. The sweet potato is a great surprise as it complements the sweet crabmeat. Meyer lemon creates the right balance between sweetness and sourness in the citrus world. Its chopped rind can be used as a salad topping.

Serves 4

Ingredients

1 medium sweet potato, boiled and mashed

4 to 6 ounces crabmeat lump, preferably Dungeness, picked over

2 teaspoons finely chopped fresh cilantro

Salt to taste

2 tablespoons all-purpose flour

2 cloves garlic, minced

½ teaspoon lemon zest

1½ cups fresh breadcrumbs, or as needed

2 tablespoons vegetable oil for frying, or as required

2 tablespoons grapeseed oil

Juice of 1 Meyer lemon

1 teaspoon honey

Pinch of white pepper powder

1 teaspoon mango powder

1 teaspoon ginger juice

1 cup diced mixed peppers, lightly grilled

2 cups arugula leaves, rinsed and dried

Directions

In a mixing bowl, combine sweet potatoes, crabmeat, cilantro, salt, flour, garlic and lemon zest and mix well.

Spread the breadcrumbs on a plate in a single layer.

Make 1½-inch to 2-inch patties with the crabmeat mixture and lightly press into the breadcrumbs to coat evenly.

Heat the oil in a non-stick pan over medium heat. Cook the crab cakes in batches until golden brown and cooked through. Remove with a slotted spoon and drain on paper towels.

In a small mixing bowl, combine oil, lemon juice, honey, white pepper, mango powder and ginger juice and mix well.

In a salad bowl, combine the grilled peppers and arugula, drizzle with the oil and lemon dressing and toss to mix well. Top with crab cakes and serve.

Family Favourite Peach Frittata

This breakfast favourite never fails to impress my family. The best part of cooking this is the surprise element I can throw in. While making it in a big batch, you can whisk the ricotta cheese with the eggs and cook in a baking pan in the oven. Adding peaches or another fruit to this frittata makes this recipe memorable.

Serves 4

Ingredients

3 tablespoons vegetable or canola oil, divided

1 medium red onion, chopped

1 medium tomato, chopped

½ cup peas, thawed (if frozen)

1 teaspoon cumin seeds

Salt to taste

6 whole eggs

¾ cup cooked long-grain rice

1 medium ripe but firm peach, pitted and chopped

1 tablespoon mango powder

Freshly ground black pepper

2 tablespoons ricotta cheese

½ cup rucola leaves, rinsed and dried

Directions

In a small skillet, heat oil over medium heat. Add onion, tomato, peas and cumin seeds with a pinch of salt, stir for a minute. Remove from heat and set aside.

Heat oil in a large skillet over medium heat.

In a mixing bowl, combine eggs, rice, half of the onion-tomato mixture, peach, mango powder, salt and freshly ground black pepper.

Pour into the skillet and add ricotta cheese in a single layer as the egg begins to set. Reduce the heat to low, cover and cook for 1 to 2 minutes, until well set.

Cut into slices, top with rucola leaves and the remaining onion-tomato mix and serve hot.

Green Mango and Shrimp Curry

Green mango and coconut are two contrasting flavours, which come together very nicely to form this satiny sweet, spicy and sour curry.

You can also use this recipe for white fish or poultry instead of shrimp.

Serves 4 to 6

Ingredients

15 to 20 shrimp, deveined, shells on

1 teaspoon turmeric

Juice of 1 lemon

1 firm green mango, peeled, pitted and coarsely chopped

½ cup grated coconut

1 tablespoon mango powder

1 teaspoon smoked paprika

3 to 4 dried red chillies

2 tablespoons vegetable oil

1 medium red onion, finely chopped

1 cup coconut milk

Salt to taste

Directions

In a mixing bowl, combine the prawns, ½ teaspoon turmeric and lemon juice and gently mix to coat well.

In a small saucepan, bring 1 cup of water and green mango to a boil on high heat. Add grated coconut, mango powder, the remaining turmeric, paprika and red chillies and cook for 4 to 5 minutes, until the flavours are well combined. Add more water if required. Transfer the mixture to a blender and process to a fine puree. Strain and set aside.

In a medium skillet, heat oil over medium heat. Add the onion and stir continuously until it's golden brown. Add the green mango mixture, the prawns and coconut milk and cook for 4 to 5 minutes, until the sauce is thick, and the prawns are cooked through. Season with salt and serve hot with steamed rice.

Crispy Okra with Mango Powder Spice Mix

This quick side dish is a good substitute for French fries. I like to gift small bags of this extremely aromatic roasted spice mix to friends. Care needs to be taken while roasting the whole spices as they turn bitter if burnt or overcooked. It is very important to add the powdered spices while blending the mix and not while roasting as they burn fast.

Serves 4

Ingredients

1-inch cinnamon stick

2 star anise

1 teaspoon cumin seeds

1 teaspoon black peppercorns

1 teaspoon fennel seeds

1 teaspoon chilli powder

1 tablespoon mango powder

1 teaspoon sweet paprika

1 pound tender okra

2 tablespoons rice flour

Salt to taste

Cooking oil for deep frying

Directions

Preheat the oven to 150°F.

On a sheet pan, lay out the cinnamon, star anise, cumin, black peppercorns and fennel. Dry roast in the oven for 8 to 10 minutes until fragrant. Remove and cool to room temperature.

Transfer the dry-roasted ingredients to a spice grinder and process to a fine powder. Strain the mixture, add chilli powder, mango powder and sweet paprika and mix well. Store in an airtight container.

Wash the okra and pat dry completely. Trim off the ends and slice thinly lengthwise.

In a mixing bowl, gently toss the okra slices in rice flour and sprinkle with salt.

Heat the oil in a skillet to 350°F. Deep-fry the okra until golden brown, remove with a slotted spoon and drain on paper towels.

Place the okra in a serving bowl and sprinkle with the spice mixture. Gently toss to coat well. Serve immediately.

Vetiver and Green Mango Shrub

Shrubs is a term used for mixed drinks, where vinegar is added to impart a subtle sourness. Vetiver is a bunchgrass with a cooling and refreshing taste and aroma that makes it a popular drink during Indian summers.

Serves 4

Ingredients

1 cup sugar

2 teaspoons mango powder

½ teaspoon vetiver syrup

2 tablespoons apple cider vinegar

1 teaspoon coriander seeds

2 ripe but firm green mangoes, pitted and julienned

Oxalis leaves for garnish

Directions

In a small saucepan, combine sugar, mango powder, vetiver syrup, apple cider vinegar, coriander seeds and ½ cup water and cook, stirring constantly until the sugar dissolves. Remove from heat and let the flavours steep at room temperature. Strain and divide the mixture into 4 glasses.

Add julienned green mangoes, crushed ice and top with chilled sparkling water. Garnish with oxalis leaves and serve.

Strawberry and Vanilla Cream with Meringue

Strawberries and cream is a classic combination, but meringue adds a delicate crunch. Whenever we add sugar or other flavourings to fruits, they release their juices, which turn syrupy and add another layer of taste—going well with the sugar and mango powder.

Serves 4

Ingredients

3 egg whites

¾ cup sugar, plus 2 tablespoons

½ vanilla bean

½ teaspoon pink colouring

2 cups strawberries, hulled and halved

1 teaspoon mango powder

½ cup whipping cream

Directions

Preheat the oven to 200°F.

Line a baking sheet with parchment paper.

Combine egg whites, ¾ cup sugar and half the vanilla bean seeds in a mixing bowl. Heat the mixture in a double boiler until the sugar dissolves, about 2 to 3 minutes.

Remove from the boiler, beat with a mixer on medium-high speed until stiff peaks form, about 5 to 7 minutes. Add pink colouring and beat well.

Fill the mixture into a piping bag and squeeze it out in the shape of a meringue onto the prepared baking sheet.

Bake in the oven for 1 hour until the outside is crisp but inside is still soft. Remove from the oven and cool on wire rack.

In a medium bowl, toss the strawberries with mango powder and 2 tablespoons sugar. Let it stand until it's syrupy, at least 10 minutes, tossing occasionally.

Mix the whipping cream in a bowl with the remaining vanilla.

In a serving bowl, lightly crush the meringue. Top with strawberries and vanilla cream and serve.

Mustard

Mustard

Mustard (*Brassica nigra*) belongs to the Cruciferae family, producing black mustard seeds; white or yellow seeds come from Brassica alba, while brown or oriental mustard from Brassica juncea.

Historical evidence indicates that mustard was grown during the Indus Valley civilisation and Sumerian and Sanskrit texts list it around 3000 BC. It is considered the smallest of all seeds on earth, about 3mm in diameter, with holy references in various religions. Jesus mentions mustard seeds in comparison to the kingdom of God in the Bible, Buddha references mustard seeds in his teachings and Jewish texts compare the universe to the size of the seed to teach humility.

Native to the temperate regions of Europe, the Romans were the first to export mustard to France. In England, chefs of King Richard II wrote about mustard in their cookbooks. It was introduced to the US in the 1904 St. Louis World Fair as a hot dog condiment.

Mild white mustard grows wild in North Africa and the Mediterranean region; brown seeds originated in the Himalayas and are grown for commercial use in India, Canada, the UK, the US and Denmark. Black seeds are grown in Chile, Argentina as well as the US.

One of the first domesticated crops, mustard is an annual herb. Planted in the months of September and October, the seedlings appear soon afterwards and within four to five weeks, mustard plants cover the ground. Flower buds can be seen in five weeks and yellow flowers, a distinct feature, appear within the week. The longer they flower, the greater the yield. Flowers produce dark red-brown dark seeds in pods.

The harvesting period is February through March, when the seed has turned yellow-green and hard, but before fully ripened. Mustard plants are dried in the sun and threshed with a stick. Black seeds are spicy and brown seeds are less pungent.

Mustard is an important ingredient in the mustard condiment, mayonnaise, barbecue and hollandaise sauces. The heat of the condiment depends on the kind of seed used, way of preparation and other ingredients.

The leaves have a peppery flavour and do well for sautéing and stewing. Younger leaves are good in salads while the older ones need to be cooked. They are often included in mesclun with milder leaves like lettuce.

Whole mustard has no aroma; grinding releases its pungent smell and when heated, the aroma becomes earthy. When chewed, the flavour of whole mustard can range from bitter and strong for brown and black seeds, to sweet for white seeds. The flowers can also be used as a garnish.

In northern India and Nepal, the seeds are used as a spice and planted to grow greens, which are cooked as a popular vegetarian preparation called sarson ka saag.

Grinding and mixing seeds with water, vinegar or other liquids makes the condiment, while pressing makes mustard oil. The leaves are known as mustard greens.

In Indian food, brown mustard is used—dry roasted in clarified butter to bring out the nutty flavour. Brown mustard is essential to the Bengali spice mix paanch phoron. Mustard oil made from these seeds is golden and pungent. It is heated to smoking point to reduce the strong aroma and then cooled for use.

In Vietnam, the leaves are used for wrapping pork, shrimp and herb stuffing. Young tender leaves are used in salads in Japan and also in Europe. Shredded leaves are used as a garnish for root vegetables.

Coconut Chicken Soup with Mustard

Mustard Dips

Grilled Chicken in Smoky Mustard Oil

Steamed Apple Butter Herring

Ginger-Scented Creamy Mustard Greens

Tamarind Mustard Rice

Fermented Carrot and Mustard Drink

White Chocolate and French Mustard Cake

Coconut Chicken Soup with Mustard

For me, this is not just a soup, but also a quick dinner when I add some quinoa or rice to it. This soup is mild, but when I make it for myself, I add hot sauce or green chillies while blending the onions and garlic. You can also add leftover vegetables to it.

Serves 4

Ingredients

2 tablespoons unsalted butter

1 large red onion, finely chopped

1-inch piece of ginger, minced

2 cloves garlic, chopped

1 cup coarsely chopped button mushrooms

2-inch piece of fresh turmeric, minced

1 tablespoon palm sugar

1 pound thin chicken breast strips

Salt to taste

3 cups coconut milk

1 tablespoon Dijon mustard

Mustard cress for garnishing

Directions

Heat the butter in a medium heavy-bottom pan over medium heat. Add the onion, ginger and garlic and cook until the onion becomes translucent. Add the mushrooms and fresh turmeric and continue to cook on low heat for about 2 to 3 minutes. Add palm sugar and stir to combine the flavours.

Transfer to a blender, process until smooth, and pour back into the pan. Add chicken and stir until well-coated. Add salt, coconut milk and mustard and bring to a boil on high heat. Reduce the heat, cover and simmer until the chicken is cooked through and the soup has reached the desired consistency, about 8 to 10 minutes.

Ladle into soup bowls, garnish with mustard cress and serve with crusty bread.

Mustard Dips

While I was developing a recipe for mustard dips, we decided to offer our guests a few options to incorporate the versatility of mustard when combined with various ingredients. This is a great opportunity to be creative and come up with unusual combinations to offer at your party.

Ingredients

Mustard Almond Dip
1 cup black mustard seeds, lightly roasted
¼ cup almonds, blanched, skinned and pureed
½ cup honey
1 teaspoon black pepper
¼ cup warm water
Salt to taste

Mustard Mint Dip
1 cup black mustard seeds
¼ cup grated coconut
1 cup mint leaves
¼ cup warm water
Salt to taste

Mustard Red Chilli Dip
1 cup Dijon mustard
¼ cup maple syrup
¼ cup Chilli paste
2 tablespoons apple cider vinegar
¼ cup warm water
Salt to taste

Mustard Turmeric Dip
1 cup yellow mustard seeds
½ cup sliced fresh turmeric
Salt to taste

Directions

To make each dip, soak the ingredients for an hour.

Transfer to a blender and process to desired consistency. Serve with fresh rucola leaves, crusty bread and olive oil.

Grilled Chicken in Smoky Mustard Oil

Smoking mustard oil helps reduce its pungency and fragrance, while the subtleness of orange juice lends another dimension to the flavour profile. When I'm entertaining at home, I generally sear the chicken and keep it ready, then just pop it into a preheated oven to get the dish ready fast. I enjoy entertaining when I can get maximum flavour with minimal effort.

Serves 4

Ingredients

3 tablespoons mustard oil

Juice of 1 lemon

1 tablespoon white wine vinegar

2 tablespoons orange juice

1 teaspoon cumin powder

1 teaspoon white pepper

Salt to taste

4 chicken breasts, cut in half

3 to 4 medium tomatoes, cut into half

8 to 10 French beans, slit lengthwise and cut into half

1 zucchini, cut into batons

1 carrot, cut into batons

Cooking oil, as needed

Directions

Heat the mustard oil to smoking in a small skillet over medium heat. Remove from heat and let it cool. Whisk in lemon juice, vinegar, orange juice, cumin powder, white pepper and salt.

Preheat the oven to 475°F.

Divide the oil mix into 2 mixing bowls. In one bowl add chicken and toss to coat. Let the chicken marinate for 30 minutes.

In the other bowl, add vegetables and toss to coat.

Heat a grill pan over medium heat and spray with cooking oil. Add chicken and vegetables and cook for about 3 to 4 minutes, turning for even cooking.

Place the pan in the oven and cook for 10 to 12 minutes.

Remove from heat and arrange on a serving platter. Serve with mustard red chilli dip.

Steamed Apple Butter Herring

A very healthy and simple dish, firm fish works better in this recipe. Marinating the fish in smooth creamy apple butter lends it a velvety texture. This can also be used as a spread.

Serves 4

Ingredients

3 to 4 red apples, cored and sliced

Pinch of salt, plus more to taste

1 teaspoon cinnamon powder

1 green chilli, split

Juice of 1 lemon

1 teaspoon turmeric powder

3 tablespoons mustard oil

2 to 3 boneless herring or cod steaks, washed and patted dry

2 cups steamed rice

Directions

In a slow cooker, add the apples with 2 tablespoons water and cook for at least 3 to 4 hours, checking at intervals to make sure the fruit doesn't stick to the bottom.

Transfer to a mixing bowl and using a wooden spoon, mash into an apple sauce.

Pour the blended sauce back into the slow cooker with salt, cinnamon powder and green chilli. Cook to a soft butter consistency.

In a mixing bowl, combine apple butter, lemon juice, turmeric powder, mustard oil and salt and gently rub into the fish. Let it marinate for 15 to 20 minutes.

Place the fish in a steamer and cook until tender and flaky. Serve with steamed rice.

Ginger-Scented Creamy Mustard Greens

A winter favourite, combining the greens with green chilli and ginger boosts its flavour. This is a versatile base that can be used for cooking seafood, meats or poultry. Broccoli rabe or spinach is a good substitute for the mustard greens.

Serves 4

Ingredients

2 tablespoons mustard oil

1 large red onion, finely chopped

2 to 3 cloves garlic, chopped

1-inch piece of ginger, finely chopped

2 green chillies, such as serrano, split and coarsely chopped

1 pound fresh mustard leaves, blanched and pureed

½ pound spinach leaves, blanched and pureed

½ cup vegetable stock

Salt to taste

2 tablespoons cornmeal

Directions

Heat mustard oil to smoking in a heavy-bottom pan over medium heat. Reduce the heat to low, add onion, garlic, ginger, 1 green chilli, mustard and spinach purees, stock, salt and cornmeal and cook. Stir occasionally until the flavours are well blended and the mixture becomes thick and creamy.

Garnish with the remaining green chilli and serve hot with flatbread.

Tamarind Mustard Rice

The sourness from tamarind paste adds a beautiful contrast to rice tempered with mustard seeds and green chilli, while palm sugar balances it out with a sweet touch. A good substitute for tamarind paste is lemon juice. Turmeric powder adds a deep golden glow to this rice dish that graces your dinner table.

Serves 4

Ingredients

1 tablespoon mustard oil

1 medium red onion, finely chopped

2 cloves garlic, minced

1 teaspoon black mustard seeds

3 cups cooked rice

1 tablespoon tamarind paste

1 teaspoon turmeric powder

1 tablespoon palm sugar

Salt to taste

Fresh cilantro for garnish

Directions

In a medium saucepan, heat mustard oil over medium heat until smoky. Reduce the heat to low and add onion, garlic and mustard seeds. Cook until the onions are translucent, about 3 to 4 minutes.

Add the rice, tamarind paste, turmeric, sugar and salt and stir to coat the rice evenly. Cook for 2 to 3 minutes until the flavours are well combined.

Garnish with fresh cilantro and serve hot with Greek yogurt.

Fermented Carrot and Mustard Drink

This is a very traditional method for making pickles and fermented drinks in India, where ground mustard seeds help in the fermentation process and create a sour taste. This drink is really prized in winters. Many times, black carrots are used in this recipe. I generally remove the green chilli from the mixture before serving; there is a hint of spiciness nevertheless. This drink can be made in a low heated oven.

Serves 4

Ingredients

6 carrots, cut into batons

1 small beetroot, peeled and coarsely chopped

1 green chilli, such as serrano, split

1 tablespoon palm sugar

3 tablespoons mustard powder

1 tablespoon black salt, or to taste

Directions

In a sterilised pitcher, combine carrots, beet, green chilli, 6 to 8 cups water, sugar, mustard powder and black salt and cover with a muslin cloth. Place in sunlight for 3 days. Stir with a sterilised spoon every day.

Serve at room temperature or chilled over ice.

White Chocolate and French Mustard Cake

This dense moist cake is perfect for teatime or as a dessert. You can also incorporate fruits such as pineapple, raspberry and peaches. You can also try this recipe with whole wheat flour and even add ¼ cup oats to make a healthier version.

Serves 4 to 6

Ingredients

1 cup unsalted butter at room temperature, plus more for greasing

2 cups self-rising flour, plus more for dusting

1 cup sugar

4 eggs

1 cup white chocolate, roughly chopped and melted in a double boiler

2 tablespoons French mustard

1 teaspoon vanilla extract

1 teaspoon star anise powder

Directions

Preheat the oven to 350°F.

Grease a 8½×4½-inch baking pan, dust with flour and set aside.

In a mixing bowl, beat butter and sugar with an electric mixer on high speed until light and fluffy. Incorporate one egg at a time into the mixture. Then add white chocolate, mustard, vanilla and star anise powder and beat well.

Gradually add flour, beating just enough until well combined, taking care not to overmix.

Pour into the greased baking pan and bake until a toothpick inserted in the centre of the cake comes out clean, about 1 hour.

If the cake begins to brown too fast, cover with aluminium foil to avoid burning.

Cool on a wire rack and serve with a jam of your choice.

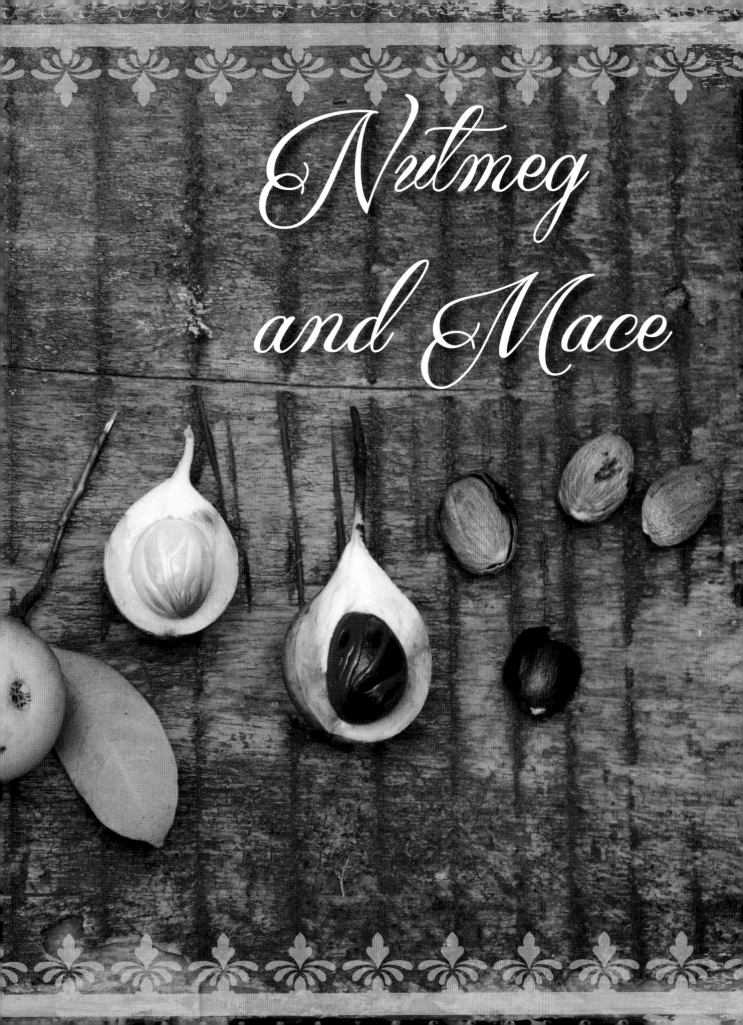

Nutmeg
and Mace

Nutmeg and Mace

Nutmeg (*Myristica fragrans*) is the spice obtained from the evergreen tree originally from the Banda Islands in Indonesia, where it is known as pala. Also found in Malaysia, the Caribbean and the southern Indian state of Kerala, nutmeg came to Indians' attention in the 17th century during their trade with Indonesia.

In medieval Europe, nutmeg was a valued and costly spice used as a seasoning, a preservative, and for its medicinal properties, highly prized as it was believed to help ward off the plague.

Nutmeg trade was controlled by the Arabs during the Middle Ages, but by the early 1500s, the Europeans took control of the islands in Indonesia. At present, the major producers of nutmeg are Indonesia and Grenada. It is also grown in India and Penang in Malaysia.

Nutmeg is the dried egg-shaped seed of the tropical tree, while the dried lacy red aril covering the seed is mace. The only tropical fruit that produces two different spices, nutmeg can be harvested seven to nine years from planting. Flowers appear in eight years; half the trees that are male do not produce fruit.

The harvesting period is from July to August. When the fruit is ripe, it turns yellow, the pulpy pericarp splits and at times naturally falls to the ground. Enclosed is a purple-brown seed surrounded by a crimson aril. They are collected immediately to avoid discolouration of the fruit.

The nut is removed by manually opening the pods; the mace is removed with a small knife from the base of the nutmeg. Otherwise, the pods are tipped to let the nut fall to a sloping floor or soaked in water for up to 12 hours, so that it can be squeezed to extract the nut.

Mace is pressed by hand to flatten and dried in the sun on mats for two to four hours. In Grenada, mace is cured in the dark for a few months, which results in the premium-quality pale yellow mace—the bigger the size, the better the price. It is then graded and packed.

The seeds are dried in the sun for about a week until they are dry enough that they rattle when shaken. The whole seed with the kernel inside can be sold as is—the dried nuts store well for a long time. To shell, the ends of the seeds are tapped with a mallet, not the sides as that might damage the kernel. They can be cracked with a machine too, the nutmeg is then sorted to remove broken ones. The quality of nutmeg depends on the size and the unbroken ones are of a higher quality; washing, grading and drying processes for the nutmeg to reach desired moisture content also influence the quality. The moisture level in wet nutmeg is more than mace and they are dried separately as mace ace takes 4–5 days while nutmeg takes 10–12 days. The sun does not ensure uniform drying; mechanically drying nutmeg ensures better appearance, a great aroma and flavour.

Nutmeg is only used in ground or powder form but once ground, it loses flavour fast so it should be grated just before use. The trees also produce essential oil, nutmeg butter and oleoresins—a mixture of resins and oil.

With similar sensory characteristics to nutmeg, mace has a more delicate flavour and gives light recipes a bright orange colour. In comparison, ground or grated nutmeg imparts a woody and sweeter flavour of cloves.

In Indonesia, nutmeg is used in spicy soups, meat gravies, stews and steaks. The flesh of the fruit is seasoned with sugar syrup or a dry sugar coating to make a popular sweet called manisan. The fruit is used in Grenada and Indonesia to make jam and candy. In Malaysian cuisine, nutmeg rind is used for sweet recipes and is blended for fresh, green and tangy nutmeg juice or boiled to make a sweet brown juice. And in Kerala, grated nutmeg goes into meat recipes, chutneys, pickles and desserts.

The Indian spice mix garam masala also includes a small quantity of nutmeg and Japan includes nutmeg in the curry powder. It is also used in savoury Indian Mughlai dishes and Middle Eastern cooking.

Both nutmeg and mace are used in European cuisine, in potato recipes, meats, soups and baked goods. Nutmeg is an important flavour for mulled wine, cider and the traditional eggnog. In the US, nutmeg is used in pumpkin pie and other squash preparations.

The essential oils are used for fragrances, beverages, food flavouring and in products like toothpaste and cough syrups. Semi-solid and red-brown in colour, nutmeg butter has an almost similar taste and aroma and is used as a substitute for cocoa butter as well as an industrial lubricant.

Spinach, Corn and Shrimp Soup

Purple Yam and Potato Rosti

Comforting Chicken Tarts

Creamy Parmesan Cheese Noodles

Mace and Black Pepper Apple Cider

Spinach, Corn and Shrimp Soup

Who says healthy soups have to be boring? This full-bodied, wholesome shrimp soup is comforting, with a hint of mace that adds to its warmth. Coconut milk gives it a nice creamy texture and some sweetness.

Serves 4

Ingredients

2 cups fish stock

1 tender corn on the cob, cut into ½ to 1-inch slices

Salt to taste

1 mace petal

2 cloves garlic, minced

1 medium white onion, sliced

10 to 12 medium shrimp, peeled and deveined

1 cup coconut milk

1 bunch spinach

Pinch of white pepper

Directions

In a medium stockpot, heat fish stock over medium heat. Add the corn, salt, mace, garlic and onion, and cook until the corn is tender, about 4 to 5 minutes.

Add shrimp and coconut milk and bring to a boil. Continue cooking until the shrimp is cooked through. Stir in the spinach and white pepper and serve hot.

Purple Yam and Potato Rosti

Sometimes, I like to start the rosti in the pan and finish it in the oven. They can be prepared halfway in advance, then finished just before serving so they are warm and crisp. Horseradish adds a wonderful layer of spiciness to this recipe. A little wasabi and pickled ginger also are great additions for a different version.

Serves 4

Ingredients

½ pound purple yam, peeled and grated

½ pound purple potato, peeled and grated

1 green chilli, such as serrano, minced

1 tablespoon horseradish sauce

1 teaspoon cardamom powder

Pinch of freshly grated nutmeg

Salt to taste

Juice of 1 lemon

3 tablespoons butter, or as required

Mint leaves for garnish

Directions

In a mixing bowl, combine purple yam, potato, green chilli, horseradish sauce, cardamom, nutmeg, salt and lemon juice and mix well.

Melt 2 tablespoons butter in a cast-iron skillet over medium heat. Place the yam and potato mixture on it and press to flatten. Cook for a minute until the bottom begins to brown. Smear one tablespoon of butter on top and gently flip to cook the other side. Continue to cook until evenly browned on both sides.

Remove from heat, cut into pieces and garnish with mint leaves. Serve with chutney or dip of your choice.

Comforting Chicken Tarts

A little nutmeg in the tart shell gives this recipe an edge over regular ones, but the shell can always have a unique flavour added for a surprise. I generally make tarts in large quantities; they can be refrigerated and reheated for a quick bite. You can use any leftover meats or chicken for the filling.

Makes 4

Ingredients

For the tarts

1½ cups flour, plus more for dusting

½ teaspoon salt

Pinch of nutmeg

1 stick unsalted butter, chilled, cut into 1-inch cubes, plus 3 tablespoons

For the filling

2 tablespoons butter

2 cloves garlic, minced

1 medium white onion, chopped

1 green chilli, finely chopped

½ cup finely chopped leeks

3 chicken thighs, deboned and finely chopped

Salt to taste

Pinch of nutmeg

½ cup chicken stock

1 tablespoon chopped parsley

6 to 8 cherry tomatoes, halved

Radish microgreens for garnish

Star fruit for garnish

Directions

To make the tarts, add flour, salt, nutmeg and butter to a food processor and gently pulse until the mixture resembles breadcrumbs. Adding a little water at a time, mix until the dough comes together. Cover with a plastic wrap and chill for at least 2 hours, preferably overnight.

Lightly flour a work surface and roll out the dough into 6-inch discs, with a $1/8$-inch thickness. Press into 4-inch tart pans with removable bases. Trim the excess dough using a paring knife and dock the bottom of the tart using a fork. Chill until ready to bake.

Preheat the oven to 350°F.

Heat butter in a saucepan over medium heat. Add garlic, onion, chilli and leeks and cook until the onion is translucent, about 3 to 4 minutes. Add chicken, salt and nutmeg and continue to cook until the flavours merge, about 2 minutes, then pour in the stock. Simmer on low heat until the liquid has been absorbed and the mixture is semi-dry, about 3 to 4 minutes.

Fill the tarts with the mixture and place on a baking sheet. Bake in the oven for 15 to 20 minutes until the tart is cooked and browned, rotating the sheet halfway through to ensure even cooking.

Garnish with parsley, cherry tomatoes and microgreens, and serve warm with a side of star fruit.

Creamy Parmesan Cheese Noodles

This sauce is a simple fix when a fast meal is needed. Cooking garlic and shallots in butter adds a rich depth to it. You can add ingredients of your choice. Nutmeg is added twice in this recipe, which echoes with flavour in every bite.

Serves 4

Ingredients

1/3 teaspoon freshly grated nutmeg, plus more for garnish

2 packs (7 ounces) rice noodles

2 tablespoons unsalted butter

2 cloves garlic

3 shallots, minced

½ cup heavy cream

¼ cup Parmesan cheese

Salt to taste

¼ cup whole milk

1/3 cup corn

1/3 cup peas, thawed (if frozen)

Directions

Bring water with salt and nutmeg to a boil over high heat. Add the noodles and cook until al dente. Drain and set aside.

In a saucepan, heat butter over medium heat. Add garlic and shallots and cook until translucent, about 3 to 4 minutes. Add cream, Parmesan and salt, cook for a minute, then pour in the milk. Continue to cook until well-combined, about a minute. Toss in the noodles, corn and peas and stir well.

Garnish with freshly grated nutmeg and serve hot.

Mace and Black Pepper Apple Cider

Generally, when I'm making apple cider at home, I start with cooking apples for a long period of time to extract maximum flavour from them. But in this recipe, I use apple juice for convenience, with similarly great results.

Serves 4

Ingredients

1/3 cup sugar

6 cups apple juice

1 mace petal

1-inch cinnamon stick

6 to 8 black peppercorns

Directions

In a large pot, over medium heat, gently caramelise the sugar until golden brown. Add the apple juice, mace, cinnamon and black peppercorns and bring to a boil.

Reduce the heat to low, cover the pot and let it simmer for at least 30 minutes.

Strain the mixture through a fine mesh sieve or cheesecloth until it is clear.

Serve hot or cold.

Pippali

Pippali

Long pepper (Piper longum), also known as Indian long pepper or pippali, is a flowering vine cultivated for its fruit, which is usually dried and used as a spice and seasoning. Long pepper has a taste similar to, but hotter and more aromatic than Piper nigrum—from which black, green and white pepper are obtained.

The word pepper has its origins from the word pippali—long pepper.

The fruit of a long pepper grows in the upward direction instead of hanging down like round pepper. It is used in combination with other herbs in Ayurvedic medicine. Believed to improve appetite and digestion, this spice has been a part of home remedies in many regions of India. In ancient Sanskrit scriptures the long pepper is extensively used it in various herbal formulations.

The peppers of the pippali plant are picked when they are still unripe, green in color. and their taste is most intense. Once harvested, the fruits are dried in the Sun until they become dark gray-ish black in color. Like Piper nigrum, the fruits contain the alkaloid piperine, which provides their pungency.

In the culinary world, long pepper is the lesser known variety. Though often used in medieval times in spice mixes like 'strong powder', it is today a very rare ingredient in European cuisines. It is an important ingredient in spice mixtures in Indian and North African cuisines, and is also commonly used in recipes of Indonesia and Malaysia. It is readily available at Indian grocery stores, where it is usually labeled pippali.

Creamy Almond Mushroom Soup

Boston Lettuce with Pippali Dressing

Soy Granules Shepherd's Pie

Spiced Tomato Rice with Poached Eggs

Black Chickpeas and Green Mango Pilaf

Strawberry Rhubarb Medley

Mint-Pippali Coffee Pudding

Creamy Almond Mushroom Soup

I love to combine different mushrooms in a single recipe because they all have different aroma and textures. Some are mild while others are richer in taste. Their combination makes a dish more interesting for the palate and the senses.

Serves 4

Ingredients

3 tablespoons butter

1 medium white onion, finely chopped

1½ pounds cremini mushrooms, cleaned and roughly chopped

5 to 6 shiitake mushrooms, cleaned and chopped

2 cloves garlic, minced

Salt to taste

½ teaspoon finely ground pippali

¼ cup blanched almonds

3 cups vegetable stock

½ cup broccoli florets

1 red Thai chilli, chopped

Directions

In a medium saucepan, heat 2 tablespoons butter over medium heat. Add the onion, stir until translucent, then add the mushrooms and garlic. Continue to cook until the mushrooms begin to dry, about 3 to 4 minutes.

Add salt, pippali, blanched almonds and vegetable stock and bring to a boil on high heat. Remove from heat and transfer to a blender. Process to a smooth mixture. Keep warm.

In a skillet, heat the remaining butter and sauté broccoli and red chilli.

Ladle the soup into bowls, top with sautéed broccoli and serve.

Boston Lettuce with Pippali Dressing

Black-eyed peas and vegetables contribute greatly to the nourishment value of this dish. The peas are rich in vitamins, proteins and fibre. Choose canned ones without any added salt.

Serves 4

Ingredients

¼ cup extra-virgin olive oil, or more if required

2 tablespoons champagne or white wine vinegar

Salt to taste

1 teaspoon coarsely ground pippali

2 cloves garlic, minced

2 shallots, minced

1 teaspoon Dijon mustard

1 tablespoon honey

1 (about ¾ pound) Boston lettuce, torn into bite-size pieces

1 medium ripe tomato, sliced

15 to 20 French beans, trimmed, blanched and cut into about 2-inch pieces

1 can (15 ounces) black-eyed peas, rinsed and drained

Directions

In a medium mixing bowl, whisk together oil, vinegar, salt, pippali, garlic, shallots, Dijon mustard and honey, until well-emulsified.

In a salad bowl, place the lettuce, tomato, French beans and black-eyed peas. Drizzle with dressing, toss to coat well and serve immediately.

Soy Granules Shepherd's Pie

A very healthy vegetarian option, this pie is easy and convenient to cook. For me, it is the adaptability of this recipe and the ease of switching ingredients, which makes it a winner. You can mix vegetables or even beans to create your version of this legendary pie.

Serves 4 to 6

Ingredients

2 tablespoons oil

1 medium red onion, finely chopped

1 star anise

2 cloves garlic

1 medium tomato, finely chopped

½ cup tomato puree

Salt to taste

1 teaspoon ground pippali

1 cup soy granules, soaked in 1 cup hot water for 30 minutes and drained

¾ cup vegetable stock

½ cup mashed potatoes

¼ cup grated Parmesan cheese

1 teaspoon white pepper

4 tablespoons heavy cream

2 tablespoons finely chopped parsley

Directions

Preheat the oven to 350°F.

Heat oil in a saucepan over medium heat. Add onion, star anise and garlic and sauté until golden brown, about 5 to 6 minutes.

Add tomato and cook for 2 to 3 minutes, until the mixture begins to dry, then add tomato puree, salt and pippali. Cook for 2 to 3 minutes before adding soy granules and vegetable stock. Continue to cook until the mixture begins to dry and the soy is cooked through, about 5 minutes.

In a separate bowl, combine mashed potatoes, Parmesan, salt, white pepper and cream.

Fill three-fourth of ramekins with the soy mixture and top with mashed potatoes. Bake in the oven for 5 to 10 minutes.

Garnish with parsley and serve hot.

Spiced Tomato Rice with Poached Eggs

A hearty dish that works well as an entrée or even as a side; you can use barley or quinoa in this recipe also. Sometimes, I make a base with pureed spinach instead of tomato for a totally new version.

Serves 4

Ingredients

4 tablespoons vegetable oil

1 medium red onion, finely chopped

1 cup long-grain basmati rice, washed, rinsed, soaked in water for 30 minutes and drained

Salt to taste

1 teaspoon ground pippali

1-inch cinnamon stick

2½ cups vegetable stock

1 medium tomato, finely chopped

1 teaspoon turmeric

1 teaspoon cumin

1-inch piece of ginger, minced

1/3 cup tomato puree

3 poached eggs

¼ cup pomegranate seeds

Fresh mint for garnish

Directions

In a saucepan, heat 2 tablespoons of oil over medium heat. Add onion, cook until translucent—2 to 3 minutes—then put in rice, salt, pippali, cinnamon and 2 cups of vegetable stock. Bring to a boil over high heat and cook until the liquid is absorbed, 8 to 10 minutes.

Reduce heat to low, cover the rice with a damp cloth and a tight-fitting lid and cook for 5 more minutes. Remove from heat and fluff with a fork.

Heat the remaining oil in a saucepan over medium heat. Add tomato, turmeric, cumin, ginger and salt. Cook until the mixture dries, about 2 to 3 minutes. Pour in the tomato puree and remaining stock and cook until the mixture reduces to a thick sauce.

Add half the rice and mix well. Top with remaining rice and gently toss together, taking care not to overmix.

Top with poached eggs, pomegranate seeds and mint leaves, and serve hot.

Black Chickpeas and Green Mango Pilaf

Green mango is used widely all over India. In season, the skin can be left on as it adds a nice crunch and texture to the bite. I like making the spice paste in large quantities so I can use it in marinades for a vibrant flavour. Alternatively, you can add seafood or grilled chicken.

Serves 4

Ingredients

4 tablespoons vegetable oil

1 medium onion, finely chopped

2 cloves garlic, minced

2 whole pippali

3 to 4 cardamom pods

½ teaspoon cloves

1-inch cinnamon stick

1 teaspoon coriander seeds 1 teaspoon turmeric

1 teaspoon red chilli powder

1 cup long-grain basmati rice, washed, rinsed, soaked in water for 30 minutes and drained

1 green mango, seeded, skinned and cut into 1 to 1½-inch pieces

½ cup boiled black chickpeas

Salt to taste

2 cups vegetable stock Fresh cilantro for garnish

Directions

In a saucepan, heat 2 tablespoons of oil over low heat. Add onion, garlic, pippali, cardamom, cloves, cinnamon and coriander and stir continuously until the onion is translucent and spices fragrant, about 5 to 6 minutes.

Transfer to a coffee grinder, add turmeric, red chilli powder and a little water as required to make a smooth paste.

In a saucepan, heat the remaining oil over medium heat. Add the onion-spice mixture and cook until fragrant, 2 to 3 minutes.

Add the rice, green mango, black chickpeas, salt and vegetable stock. Bring to a boil over high heat and cook until the liquid is absorbed, 8 to 10 minutes. Reduce heat to low, cover the rice with a damp cloth and a tight-fitting lid, and cook for 5 more minutes. Remove from heat and fluff with a fork.

Garnish with cilantro and serve hot.

Strawberry Rhubarb Medley

A great crowd-pleaser, cooking the fruit with sugar and spices enhances its flavours. You can top with lemonade or champagne to add another taste dimension.

Serves 4 to 6

Ingredients

4 tablespoons sugar, or to taste

8 to 10 strawberries, hulled and coarsely chopped

1 stalk rhubarb, finely chopped

1 cup orange juice

Pinch of cardamom powder

½ teaspoon coarsely ground pippali

Directions

Heat a saucepan over medium heat. Add sugar with ½ cup water and stir until it dissolves.

Add strawberries, rhubarb, orange juice and cardamom powder and cook until the flavours merge, 2 to 3 minutes.

Transfer to a blender and process to a fine puree.

Strain if required.

Pour into glasses over ice. Top with water, garnish with pippali and serve.

Mint-Pippali Coffee Pudding

An easy and foolproof coffee pudding, this can also be prepared in a microwave. Using heavy cream instead of milk creates a creamy denseness. This recipe can easily be made into a multi-layered pudding as a variation, by dividing the mixture into two parts—one with vanilla and the other with coffee.

Serves 4

Ingredients

½ cup sugar

2 tablespoons instant coffee, or to taste

4 tablespoons corn starch

2 ¼ cup whole milk, warm

½ teaspoon vanilla extract

½ teaspoon coarsely ground pippali

Few drops of mint extract

1 cup coarsely chopped fruits

Mint leaves for garnish

Directions

In a mixing bowl over a double boiler on medium heat, combine sugar, coffee and corn starch. Whisk in milk gradually, ensuring it doesn't form lumps. Stir in the vanilla, pippali and mint extract.

Remove from heat and pour into serving cups or glasses. Cover with plastic film directly on the surface of the pudding and chill in the refrigerator.

Top with fresh fruits and mint leaves and serve chilled.

Saffron

Saffron

Saffron is obtained from the *Crocus sativus* flower, commonly known as the saffron crocus.

Native to the Mediterranean, this perennial plant flowers in the fall. The major producer of saffron is Spain.

The plant thrives in hot and dry climate but it is capable of surviving harsh winters. It grows up to one foot prior to blooming white, non-photosynthetic leaves known as cataphylls, which appear as a cover for the real blade-like green leaves that sprout in spring. Purple buds appear in the autumn, followed by sweet-smelling bright lilac-mauve-purple flowers in October. Each flower has a style with three prongs, each ending with a crimson stigma. It is from this stigma that saffron spice is derived, three from each flower. Threads of saffron are collected from these styles and stigmata are dried to be used as a spice.

Flowers bloom within a couple of weeks, blossoming at dawn and wilting as the day progresses, so have to be picked quickly. The threads are roasted over a low fire on a sieve so they become dry and brittle; the colour changes from deep red to orangish. Approximately 150 flowers yield 1 g of dry saffron threads. It is considered the world's most expensive spice.

Saffron gets its golden hues from the pigment crocin, and its trade and usage have been recorded in historical writings since the 7th century BC. In cooking, it adds a rich, pungent, musky-floral aroma and a taste that is warm, earthy and at the same time slightly bitter. The saffron is soaked in liquid, water, milk or such, which is added to impart colour and aroma to soups, stews, desserts and marinades. Too much saffron can make the taste bitter so it should be used in appropriate amounts.

Dried stamen or threads need to be stored in a cool dark place in an airtight container. If stored appropriately, it can keep well for up to three years.

Saffron is also considered auspicious and is used in celebrations, festivals and to mark good beginnings.

Coconut Saffron Clam Soup

Summer Watermelon Salad

Apple Cider Roast Chicken

Smoky Mashed Potatoes

Almond Milk Rice Pilaf

Honey, Tangerine and Saffron Marmalade

Sparkling Saffron Apple Fizz

Ginger Saffron Yogurt Cake

Coconut Saffron Clam Soup

Creamy saffron and coconut milk complement the delicate flavours of briny fresh clams in a traditional chowder-like soup. Its consistency can be adjusted to your preference by adding corn starch.

Serves 4

Ingredients

1 tablespoon mustard oil

1 medium red onion, thinly sliced

2 cloves garlic, minced

1-inch cinnamon stick

2 bay leaves

1 green chilli, such as serrano

1 cup coconut milk

½ cup dry white wine

1 teaspoon lemon juice

1 teaspoon turmeric

Salt to taste

6-8 Saffron threads, soaked in 2 tablespoons warm milk

2 pounds clams, such as Littleneck or Manila, rinsed and scrubbed

Fresh cilantro for garnish

Directions

Heat oil in a pan on high heat until it begins to smoke. Reduce the heat to medium and add the onion, garlic, cinnamon and bay leaves. Stir continuously until the onion is translucent, 2 to 3 minutes.

Stir in the chilli, coconut milk and wine, then add lemon juice, turmeric, salt and the saffron mixture. Continue to cook, stirring, until the flavours merge, about 2 to 3 minutes.

Reduce the heat to low and add the clams. Cover with a lid and let it steam until the clams open, about 5 minutes. Discard the clams that have not opened or the ones with broken shells.

Garnish with cilantro and serve immediately.

Summer Watermelon Salad

A simple dressing of olive oil and saffron strikes the right flavour balance in this refreshing green salad with melon, rucola and sharp, tangy feta. Lightly roasted nuts such as pine nuts or almonds add a nice crunch to each bite.

Serves 4 to 6

Ingredients

Juice of 1 lemon

1 tablespoon agave syrup, or to taste

Pinch of saffron, soaked in 1 tablespoon warm water

1 teaspoon ginger juice

2 cloves garlic, minced

Salt to taste

3 tablespoons olive oil

1 cup rucola leaves, washed

½ medium watermelon, rind removed, seeded and sliced

½ cup crumbled feta or ricotta cheese

Directions

In a medium mixing bowl, whisk together lemon juice, agave syrup, saffron mixture, ginger juice, garlic and salt. Gently drizzle olive oil until the mixture is emulsified and creamy.

Combine the rucola, watermelon and cheese in a large salad bowl. Drizzle with the dressing and serve.

Apple Cider Roast Chicken

This is a simple yet delicious golden roast chicken marinated in saffron, clarified butter, salt and pepper. Roasting with wine and apple cider helps moisten and tenderise the chicken. If you want to avoid using wine, then apple cider juice also does the trick.

Serves 4

Ingredients

3 tablespoons clarified butter

½ teaspoon saffron,
soaked in 1 tablespoon warm water

1 teaspoon salt, or to taste

½ teaspoon white pepper

Juice of 1 lemon, or to taste

½ teaspoon turmeric

1 whole medium chicken, giblets and excess
fat removed, rinsed and patted dry

12 to 15 baby potatoes, quartered

10 cloves garlic

½ cup dry white wine

1 cup apple cider

Mint leaves for garnish

Directions

Preheat the oven to 450°F.

In a small mixing bowl, add clarified butter, saffron, salt, pepper, lemon juice and turmeric and mix well.

Put chicken, potatoes and garlic in a large bowl and marinate with the saffron mixture.

In a baking pan with raised edges, place the chicken in the centre and scatter the garlic and potatoes around it. Pour in the wine and apple cider and roast until the chicken is golden brown and cooked through, about 1 hour. The instant-read thermometer should read 165°F when inserted in the thickest part.

Garnish with mint leaves and serve hot.

Smoky Mashed Potatoes

Classic buttery and creamy mashed potatoes with smoked Gouda is a comforting and satisfying side dish anytime. The combination of the smoked cheese, citrusy yuzu and spicy horseradish brings together diverse flavours; more yuzu makes it more lemony, which pairs well with seafood. This recipe can be made using sweet potatoes, cauliflower or squash.

Serves 4

Ingredients

3 pounds Yukon Gold potatoes, peeled and cut into 1-inch pieces

Salt to taste

1 teaspoon horseradish

¼ pound smoked Gouda, grated

1 teaspoon saffron threads, soaked in 1 tablespoon warm water

2 tablespoons yuzu juice

2 tablespoons sour cream

Microgreens for garnish

Directions

In a medium saucepan, place potatoes in enough salted water to cover by at least 2 inches and bring to a boil on high heat. Reduce the heat to low, cover and simmer until the potatoes are cooked through, about 10 to 12 minutes. Remove from heat and drain.

Press through a ricer into a large saucepan, or use a potato masher and mash until smooth. Add horseradish, Gouda, saffron, yuzu and sour cream. Season with salt if required.

Garnish with microgreens of your choice and serve.

Almond Milk Rice Pilaf

A fluffy, saffron-hued pilaf with crunchy almonds, this dish is flavourful and elegant for an evening of entertaining. Almond milk adds a rich nutty taste and a natural sweetness.

Serves 4

Ingredients

2 tablespoon vegetable oil

3 shallots, minced

1 cup long-grain basmati rice, washed, rinsed, soaked in water for 30 minutes and drained

1 teaspoon saffron threads

3 to 5 cardamom pods, lightly crushed

Salt to taste

2 cups unsweetened almond milk

¼ cup slivered almonds

Directions

In a saucepan, heat oil over medium heat. Add shallots and cook until translucent, 2 to 3 minutes.

Add rice, saffron, cardamom, salt and almond milk. Bring to a boil over high heat and continue to cook until the liquid is absorbed, 8 to 10 minutes. Reduce heat to low, cover the rice with a damp cloth and a tight-fitting lid and cook for 5 more minutes.

Stir in almonds and fluff with a fork.

Serve hot.

Honey, Tangerine and Saffron Marmalade

Home-made marmalade is a great way to preserve the abundant bounty of tangerines in season. The sweet and complex flavours of citrus fruits and juices work well in recipes like this. Saffron enhances both colour and flavour. It's great for toasts or even as a filling for cakes.

Makes about 2½ cups

Ingredients

10 to 12 tangerines

3 cups orange juice

1 teaspoon saffron

1-inch piece of ginger, finely chopped

½ teaspoon lemon zest

½ cup sugar, or to taste

1 cup honey

Directions

Peel the tangerines and cut the rind into thin strips, lengthwise. Reserve.

Coarsely chop the tangerines and discard the seeds, if any.

In a medium pot, combine tangerines with orange juice and bring to a boil. Reduce heat to medium, add saffron, ginger and lemon zest and simmer until the mixture becomes thick, about 10 to 12 minutes.

Add sugar and honey and continue to cook, stirring until the sugar dissolves, about 15 to 20 minutes.

Remove from heat, skim off the scum and let it cool. Store in a sterilised airtight jar in a refrigerator for up to a month.

Sparkling Saffron Apple Fizz

Fizzy apple cider is a refreshing addition to this drink alongside lime juice. Delicate strands of saffron elevate this graceful cocktail.

Serves 4

Ingredients

½ cup sugar

1 teaspoon saffron

Juice of 1 lime

4 cups sparkling apple cider, or as required

Directions

In a small saucepan, combine sugar, 1 cup water and saffron and heat over medium heat until the sugar dissolves. Remove from heat and let the flavours steep. Cool to room temperature and add lime juice.

To serve, pour the syrup into glasses over ice and top with sparkling apple cider.

Ginger Saffron Yogurt Cake

A soft fluffy cake full of the warm flavours of ginger, saffron and raisins, this cake gets its creamy texture from the yogurt.

Serves 4

Ingredients

1 cup butter, at room temperature, plus more for greasing

1¾ cup all-purpose flour, plus more for dusting

1 teaspoon baking powder

½ teaspoon baking soda

1 teaspoon ginger powder

1 cup sugar

1 cup whole milk Greek yogurt

3 medium eggs, at room temperature

1 teaspoon vanilla extract

1 teaspoon saffron, lightly roasted and mixed with 2 tablespoons warm milk

1 teaspoon lemon zest

2 tablespoons raisins

Directions

Preheat the oven to 350°F.

Grease an 8-inch baking pan and dust with flour.

In a medium mixing bowl, sift together flour, baking powder, baking soda and ginger powder.

In a large mixing bowl, whisk butter and sugar with a hand blender at medium speed. Add yogurt, continue to mix, then add one egg at a time. Mix well. Add vanilla extract, saffron mixture and lemon zest and whisk until well blended. Gradually fold in the dry ingredients and raisins, but do not overmix.

Transfer the batter to the prepared baking pan and bake in the oven for 50 to 60 minutes, until the toothpick inserted in the centre of the cake comes out clean.

Serve warm or at room temperature.

Star Anise

Star anise (*Illicium verum*) is the anise-flavoured, star-shaped pericarp of the fruit of the evergreen tree, native to Vietnam and southwest China. The word Illicium means enticing in Latin, which appropriately describes the beautiful spice with perfectly pointed five to 10 stars each and a shiny, polished brown seed. The Chinese prize star anise and believe the spice with more than eight points brings good luck; the star anise is to the Chinese what the four-leaf clover is to the Irish.

Introduced to Europe in the 17th century, the seeds of the star anise contain some flavour but most of the taste is really in the star-shaped case. It is commercially produced in Japan and India; but it should not be confused with the toxic and inedible Japanese star anise fruit, which it closely resembles.

A member of the magnolia family, the bright green bushy tree sports broad lower leaves and feathery upper leaves. Small yellow-white flowers with a pleasant aroma grow in clusters shaped like umbrellas in the summer and bear star-shaped fruits. It is harvested just before it ripens while it is still green and sun-dried until it becomes dark in colour and develops a woody flavour and aroma. The harvesting period is between March and May.

Star anise contains anethole, which gives it the liquorice flavour, but otherwise, the two are not related. Star anise has a slightly bitter taste compared to anise and is cheaper too. It is added as a spice whole or ground to a red-brown powder. The latter is strong and should be used sparingly. It adds a fennel-anise tangy warmth with a numbing sweet and pungent aftertaste.

Star anise is used in spice mixes like the Chinese five-spice and Indian garam masala, for meat and bean stews, cookies, cakes, fruit-based desserts as well as beverages like tea. It adds authenticity to Chinese cooking, soups, marinades, steamed poultry, and colour and flavour to marbled eggs, red-cooked chicken, duck and pork. In the West, star anise is mainly used for flavouring seafood, syrups, cordials, poaching fruit, liquor and confectionery and is a cheaper substitute for anise. It is used in pho, the Vietnamese dish, and French mulled wine.

Its non-culinary uses include addition to soap, fragrances, toothpaste and aromatherapy oils. It is also used in cough medicine and to cure digestive disorders. Star anise is considered a warming herb in China.

Stored whole or in pieces in an airtight container, out of bright light, star anise keeps for a year. Pieces of star anise are known as segments, points and sections. The ground spice loses flavour fast and should be purchased in small amounts.

Chinese Five-Spice Vegetable Soup

Summertime Lamb and Rice Salad

Creamy Puy Lentils with Lamb Shanks

Asian Tofu and Spaghetti

Tea-Infused Vegetable Pulao

Apple, Cranberry and Star Anise Chutney

Ginger-Star Anise Apple Juice

Chickpeas and Apricot Rice Pudding

Chinese Five-Spice Vegetable Soup

This comforting soup is very simple to make. If you like your soups to be light and runny, then skip the corn starch. Any vegetable combination can work well; at times, I even add fruits, which lend a sweet undertone.

Serves 4

Ingredients

For the five-spice mix

6 star anise

3 to 4 cloves

2-inch cinnamon stick

1 teaspoon black peppercorns

1½ teaspoons fennel seeds

For the soup

2 tablespoons sesame oil

2 cloves garlic, minced

1-inch piece of ginger, minced

1 tablespoon soy sauce

1 teaspoon sugar

2 to 3 medium carrots, peeled and cut into batons

1 pound French string beans, both ends removed and cut into half

2 tablespoons tomato puree

Salt to taste

4 cups vegetable stock

2 tablespoons corn starch mixed with 2 tablespoons water

Directions

Grind the five-spice ingredients in a coffee or spice grinder to a fine powder. Store in an airtight container for up to 4 to 6 weeks.

Heat oil in a wok on medium heat. Add garlic, ginger, soy sauce, sugar and 1 teaspoon five-spice mix, and cook until fragrant.

Add the carrots, beans, tomato puree and salt and stir until evenly coated. Pour in the stock and bring to a boil on high heat. Reduce heat to medium, add the corn starch mixture, stirring continuously, and cook until the soup thickens to the desired consistency.

Serve hot.

Summertime Lamb and Rice Salad

There is an abundance of squashes during summer, and you should always choose tender and smooth ones for your recipes. If you want to make this into a complete meal, add the stock and continue to cook till you get a porridge-like consistency.

Serves 4

Ingredients

4 tablespoons oil

2 cloves garlic, minced

1-inch piece of ginger, minced

1 teaspoon cumin powder

Salt to taste

8 to 10 ounces lamb, coarsely chopped

Juice of 1 lemon

1 red onion, finely chopped

2 star anise

1 cup short-grain brown rice, washed, rinsed, soaked in water for 30 minutes and drained

1 medium zucchini, diced

1 cups diced summer squash

1 tomato, sliced

Directions

Heat 2 tablespoons of oil in a skillet over medium heat. Add the garlic, ginger, cumin and salt and stir until fragrant, about 2 minutes. Put in the lamb and cook for 2 to 3 minutes, stirring constantly. Remove from heat and mix in the lemon juice.

In a large stockpot, heat the remaining oil over medium heat. Add onion and star anise and cook until the onion is translucent, about 2 to 3 minutes.

Add rice, zucchini, squash, lamb, 5 cups water and salt and bring to a boil over high heat. Cook for 15 to 20 minutes, or until the rice is al dente. Remove from heat and drain excess liquid.

Toss in the tomato and serve hot.

Creamy Puy Lentils with Lamb Shanks

The addition of lentils while cooking meats is a common tradition in the Mediterranean and Indian cuisines. It not only has high nutrition value but also lends creaminess to the lamb curry.

Serves 4

Ingredients

2 tablespoons peanut or sesame oil

5 to 6 lamb shanks

1 bay leaf

2 to 3 star anise

1 sprig fresh rosemary

2 medium red onions, finely chopped

2 tablespoons tomato paste

1-inch piece of ginger, minced

¾ cup puy lentils, rinsed, soaked in 2 cups water for 30 minutes and drained

1 teaspoon sweet paprika

Freshly ground black pepper

Salt to taste

2 tablespoons capers

2 tablespoons finely chopped parsley

Directions

Heat oil in a saucepan over medium heat. Sear lamb shanks on all sides until golden brown. Transfer to a plate and set aside.

To the same pan, add bay leaf, star anise, rosemary and onions and cook on medium heat, stirring continuously until the onions begin to caramelise and are golden, about 5 to 6 minutes. Add the tomato paste and ginger and stir well.

Add the lamb shanks and puy lentils and stir until well-coated. Put in sweet paprika, black pepper, salt and capers and mix well. Pour enough water to cover the mixture, reduce heat to low, cover and simmer until the lamb is fork-tender and the lentils cooked. Add more water if required.

Stir in the peppers, garnish with chopped parsley and serve.

Asian Tofu and Spaghetti

A quick and easy meal that can be prepared in advance for a family feast. Tofu is an extremely versatile and absorbs the flavours of ingredients well. I generally end the dish with a splash of hot sauce for a extra kick.

Serves 4

Ingredients

1 pound thin spaghetti or egg noodles

2 tablespoons sesame oil

1 star anise

16 ounces firm tofu

1 tablespoon hoisin sauce

1 tablespoon oyster sauce

1 tablespoon light soy sauce

½ teaspoon white pepper powder

Salt to taste

Garlic chives for garnish

Directions

In a large stockpot, bring salted water to a boil on high heat, add the noodles and cook until al dente, about 3 to 5 minutes. This will depend on the type of noodles you're using. Drain and set aside.

In a wok, heat the oil on medium-high heat. Add the star anise, noodles, tofu, sauces, white pepper and salt and stir well.

Garnish with garlic chives and serve hot.

Tea-Infused Vegetable Pulao

The smokiness of tea fills each bite of this vegetable pulao with richness. You can also use lentils or make it with barley. Kaffir lime leaves will add a delicious citrusy undertone.

Serves 4

Ingredients

1 tablespoon canola or vegetable oil

1 medium red onion, diced

2 to 3 star anise

1 celery stalk, trimmed and diced

½ cup diced mixed peppers

2 cups short-grain rice, washed, rinsed, soaked in water for 30 minutes and drained

Salt to taste

4 cups vegetable stock

2 black tea bags

Pickled cucumbers for garnish

Directions

In a saucepan, heat oil over medium heat. Add onion and star anise and sauté until the onion is translucent, about 2 minutes. Add celery and peppers and continue to cook.

Add rice, salt, vegetable stock and tea bags and bring to a boil on high heat until the liquid is absorbed, about 12 to 15 minutes. Reduce the heat to low, cover and cook for another 3 to 5 minutes.

Remove from heat, discard the tea bags, and serve hot with pickled cucumbers on the side.

Apple, Cranberry and Star Anise Chutney

The bold and tart taste of cranberries, apples, cider vinegar and liquorice-like star anise, all come together to create a perfect harmony of flavours. It will pair well with mains, including meats and breads. I retain the star anise as whole in this chutney because with time, it releases additional flavour that deepens the overall taste profile.

Makes about 1½ cups

Ingredients

½ cup brown sugar

1 cup dried cranberries

1 red apple, cored and finely chopped

4 tablespoons apple cider vinegar

Salt to taste

1 cup cranberry juice

2 star anise

Directions

In a medium saucepan, combine all the ingredients except star anise and bring to a boil over high heat. Reduce the heat, simmer and cook until the mixture is thick and the flavours well-combined.

Transfer to a blender and puree to a coarse mixture. Add back to the pan with star anise and cook until the flavours merge. Add more cranberry juice if required.

Remove from heat and serve hot with meats, or refrigerate in an airtight sterilised jar for up to 3 weeks.

Ginger-Star Anise Apple Juice

The bite from ginger and liquorice taste of the star anise elevates this sugar syrup to a new level. You can store it in the refrigerator and use to make desserts or sweeten drinks.

Serves 4

Ingredients

½ cup sugar

2 star anise

2-inch piece of ginger, peeled and crushed

2 ounces white rum, or as required

Juice of 2 lemons, or as required

A few dashes of Angostura bitters

2 cups apple juice

2 lime wedges, twisted

Fresh cilantro sprigs for garnish

Directions

In a small saucepan, combine sugar, 1 cup water, star anise and ginger and heat over medium heat until the sugar dissolves. Remove from heat and let the flavours steep while cooling to room temperature.

In a pitcher, mix sugar syrup as required, rum, water, lemon juice, bitters and apple juice. To serve, pour into glasses over crushed ice, and garnish with lime twists and cilantro.

Chickpeas and Apricot Rice Pudding

The rich and nutty almond milk is a great option for people who are lactose intolerant. Apricots add a natural sweetness and velvety texture to the dessert.

Serves 4

Ingredients

2 tablespoons clarified butter

3 tablespoons short-grain rice, rinsed and drained

½ cup boiled chickpeas, pureed

2 cups whole milk

1 cup almond milk

4 to 6 dried apricots, finely chopped

4 tablespoons sugar, or to taste

2 star anise

10 to 12 pistachios, finely chopped, for garnish

¼ cup fresh pomegranate seeds for garnish

Directions

In a heavy-bottom skillet, heat the clarified butter on medium heat. Add rice, chickpea puree, whole milk and almond milk, and bring to a boil on high heat, stirring continuously to ensure the milk does not burn.

Add apricots, sugar and star anise. Reduce the heat to low and simmer until the mixture becomes thick and creamy. Adjust sugar if required.

Garnish with pistachios and pomegranate seeds and serve warm.

Tamarind

Tamarind

Tamarind (*Tamarindus indica*), native to Africa, is grown in tropical regions across the globe—South Asia, Taiwan, China, northern Australia, Oman and Mexico. India is the largest producer at present. Tamarind is consumed worldwide due to its popularity as an ingredient in various cuisines. The name derives from the Arabic *tamar hindi*, meaning Indian date. Historical references are included in the writings of Marco Polo, who wrote about *tamarandi*.

Tamarind trees grow to heights of 80 feet and more with a single trunk. The leaves are arranged alternately and pinnately on either side of the stem, each with bright green elongated leaflets that fold at night.

The flower buds are pink because of the outer sepals, which fall when the flower blooms. Small five-petal yellow flowers with red-orange streaks are borne on small stalks on either side of a main stem. The brown fruit pods are curved and bulging with green flesh, soft with acid, and whitish seeds when they are underdeveloped. As they mature, the pods are filled with sharp and sour juicy brown-reddish fibrous pulp surrounding the seeds. The skin turns brittle and the pulp loses moisture naturally to become a sticky mass surrounded by fibre strands, while the brown seeds turn hard and glossy.

Even after they have matured, the pods are left on trees for further reduction of moisture content. They're harvested by pulling them off the stalk or shaking the branches to let them fall to the ground naturally. Care is taken to not damage the shell.

Tamarind is stored by removing the shell. It is pressed into balls or enclosed in barrels with sugar and covered with boiling syrup before shopping to processors. In India, the pulp (both with seeds, fibres and also at times without) is mixed with 10 per cent salt, and converted into blocks through pounding, wrapped with palm leaf and then into burlap sacks. Sun-drying or steaming the blocks helps to store well for longer periods. Whether block, concentrate or syrup, tamarind can be preserved indefinitely.

The pulp has a sweet-sour taste, fruity at times. The sourness is due to tartaric acid, and varies with the area it is grown in. Tamarind is used to add an acidic sourness or sharp flavour to curries, chutneys, marinades, pickles and preserves in Southeast Asian countries. It is also an ingredient in Worcestershire sauce. The tamarind block is used by soaking in hot water; the pulp is squeezed out and seeds and fibre removed. The concentrate is used by mixing in water. In Thailand and the Philippines, the leaves and flowers are also used. At times, even the ripe greenish pulp is used to add sourness to savoury recipes.

Chicken Meatballs with Beet-Tamarind Soup

Roasted Pumpkin and Couscous Salad

Tamarind-Flavoured Threadfin Bream

Eggplant in Tomato-Rhubarb Gravy

Baked Peppery Potatoes

Tamarind Chilli Sherbet

Tamarind and Hazelnut Fudge Brownie

Chicken Meatballs
with Beet-Tamarind Soup

Beetroot broth gives a beautiful garnet hue to this soup, while the meatballs soak in all the flavours—a fragrant floral warmth from bay leaf, combined with the pungency of peppercorns and a tart uplift from tamarind.

Serves 4 to 6

Ingredients

For the meatballs

12 ounces minced chicken breast

1 clove garlic, minced

2 tablespoons finely chopped cilantro

1 teaspoon cumin powder

1 egg, lightly beaten

1 teaspoon paprika

1 teaspoon salt

2 tablespoons breadcrumbs

For the soup

2 tablespoons oil

1 medium red onion, finely chopped

2 cloves garlic

1 bay leaf

1-inch cinnamon stick

2 medium beetroots, peeled and diced

2 tablespoons tamarind paste

1½ cups chicken stock

Salt to taste

4 scallions, coarsely chopped

Directions

To make the meatballs, mix all the ingredients together in a medium mixing bowl. Cover and let it rest in the refrigerator for at least 30 minutes.

Lightly dampen your hands and roll the mixture into 1 to 1½-inch balls. Place them in a dish, cover with plastic film and let rest in the refrigerator for another 30 minutes.

For the soup, heat oil in a medium pan over medium heat. Add onion, garlic, bay leaf and cinnamon and sauté until the onion is translucent, about 2 to 3 minutes. Add beetroot, tamarind paste, stock and salt and bring to a boil. Reduce heat and simmer. Gently transfer the meatballs into the beetroot mixture and continue to cook, cautiously turning them until cooked through.

Garnish with scallions and serve hot.

Roasted Pumpkin and Couscous Salad

In this hearty salad, pumpkin, red peppers and broccoli are roasted till tender, then tossed with warm fluffy couscous flavoured with tamarind. The vegetables can be substituted with those of your preference.

Serves 6

Ingredients

1 small butternut squash, peeled, seeded, cut into 1 to 1½-inch cubes and blanched

1 small broccoli, cut into florets

2 red peppers, cored, seeded and cubed

1 green chilli, such as serrano, minced

2 cloves garlic, minced

Salt to taste

1 teaspoon finely ground fennel seeds

4 tablespoons olive oil

Juice of 1 lemon

2 cups couscous

Freshly ground black pepper

1 tablespoon tamarind paste mixed in 1 tablespoon hot water

Directions

Preheat the oven to 375°F.

In a mixing bowl, combine squash, broccoli, peppers, green chilli, garlic, salt, fennel, 2 tablespoons oil and lemon juice. Toss to coat well.

Place on a greased baking sheet in a single layer. Bake until tender, about 20 minutes.

Meanwhile, in a mixing bowl, combine the couscous, salt, pepper and remaining oil, using a fork to evenly coat the couscous. Add 2½ cups of boiling water, give it a gentle stir with a fork and cover with a plastic film. Let the couscous stand for at least 5 minutes, then gently fluff with a fork. Stir in the tamarind.

Top the couscous with the roasted vegetables and serve hot.

Tamarind-Flavoured Threadfin Bream

A simple marinade of tamarind, chilli and garlic for slow cooking is a great way to prepare fish that is meltingly tender and moist. A pleasing centrepiece for a great meal with family and friends, the mildly flavourful threadfin bream revels in the sour hints of tamarind.

Serves 2 to 4

Ingredients

4 medium threadfin bream, scaled, gilled and gutted

Salt to taste

4 tablespoons oil

1 teaspoon chilli powder, or to taste

1 teaspoon garlic powder

1 tablespoon tamarind paste

1 medium red onion, finely chopped

3 medium tomatoes, finely chopped

1-inch piece of ginger, minced

½ cup dry white wine

¼ cup fenugreek microgreens

Directions

Using a damp kitchen towel, gently wipe the belly cavity of the fish thoroughly. Lightly season it with salt, oil, chilli powder, garlic powder and tamarind paste. Cover and let marinate at room temperature for at least 15 to 20 minutes.

In a cast-iron skillet, heat the remaining oil over medium heat. Add onion, tomatoes and ginger and gently mix. Season with salt and place fish over the mixture in a single layer. Cook for 1 to 2 minutes, then gently turn the fish over.

Add white wine, reduce the heat to low, cover and cook until the fish flakes easily with a fork, about 6 to 8 minutes.

Plate the fish, top with onion-tomato mixture and garnish with fenugreek microgreens. Serve hot.

Eggplant in Tomato-Rhubarb Gravy

The luscious tomato gravy for this deep-fried eggplant recipe is flavoured with cinnamon, tamarind, garlic and cumin. You can use Japanese eggplant too. It's important to simmer the eggplant in the sauce so it absorbs all the flavours. The sour taste of rhubarb complements the tamarind.

Serves 4

Ingredients

Vegetable oil for frying, plus 2 tablespoons

4 to 6 baby eggplants, trimmed and quartered

1 teaspoon chilli powder, or to taste

Salt to taste

1 medium red onion, finely chopped

2 cloves garlic, minced

1-inch cinnamon stick

1 bay leaf

2 medium tomatoes, finely chopped

½ cup finely chopped rhubarb

3 tablespoons tomato puree

2 tablespoons tamarind

1 teaspoon cumin powder

½ cup vegetable stock, or as required (optional)

Fresh cilantro leaves for garnish

Directions

Heat the oil in a frying pan to 350°F.

Deep-fry the eggplant until golden brown. Remove with a slotted spoon and drain on a kitchen towel. Sprinkle with chilli powder and salt.

In a skillet, heat the 2 tablespoons oil over medium heat. Sauté the onion, garlic, cinnamon and bay leaf until the onion begins to caramelise. Add a little water if it begins to burn.

Add the tomatoes and rhubarb, and cook until the mixture begins to dry. Pour in tomato puree, tamarind, cumin and mix well. Add the seasoned eggplant and toss to coat. Continue to cook until the flavours merge. If the sauce is too thick, add some vegetable stock and cook for 2 to 3 minutes to achieve desired consistency.

Garnish with cilantro and serve hot.

Baked Peppery Potatoes

Crispy baked potatoes are a welcome meal any day. Here, garlic and tamarind coat the potatoes with a rich flavour that can be tasted in every bite. Grains of paradise add a peppery note to the dish.

Serves 4 to 6

Ingredients

4 russet potatoes, scrubbed and cut into ½-inch thick rounds

2 tablespoons tamarind pulp

1 teaspoon chilli powder, or to taste

2 cloves garlic, minced

1-inch piece of ginger, minced

1 teaspoon coriander seeds, lightly crushed

1 teaspoon grains of paradise, coarsely ground

Salt to taste

2 tablespoons oil, plus more for greasing

Fresh cilantro leaves for garnish

Directions

Preheat the oven to 400°F.

In a mixing bowl, combine potatoes, tamarind pulp, chilli powder, garlic, ginger, coriander seeds, grains of paradise and salt. Drizzle oil on top and toss to coat well.

Place on a greased baking sheet in a single layer and bake until the potatoes are golden and crisp, 45 to 50 minutes.

Garnish with cilantro and serve hot with a dip of your choice.

Tamarind Chilli Sherbet

This refreshing tamarind drink is a real palate pleaser—salty, earthy, sulfurous from black salt, sweet from jaggery, sour from tamarind and spicy from chilli. You can use brown sugar instead of jaggery.

Serves 4

Ingredients

4 tablespoons tamarind pulp

4 tablespoons grated jaggery or muscovado, or to taste

Salt to taste

1 teaspoon pink salt, to taste

3 to 4 dried red chillies, broken

Directions

In a pitcher, combine all the ingredients with ½ cup warm water and mix well until the jaggery dissolves. Refrigerate to chill.

To serve, pour over ice and top with seltzer or water.

Tamarind and Hazelnut Fudge Brownie

The classic combination of chocolate and hazelnut gets a surprise twist thanks to tamarind. Each bite is sweet, earthy and sour with a nutty crunch. The use of nuts in this recipe is optional. You can add chopped candied fruits as an alternative.

Serves 4

Ingredients

½ cup unsalted butter, plus more for greasing

¾ cup whole wheat flour, plus more for dusting

10 to 12 ounces bittersweet or dark chocolate, coarsely chopped

1 cup brown sugar

4 large eggs

2 teaspoons cardamom powder

2 tablespoons tamarind paste

¼ cup hazelnuts, lightly roasted and finely chopped

Directions

Preheat the oven to 350°F.

Grease and lightly dust an 8-inch square pan.

Place butter and chocolate in the top of a double boiler or heatproof bowl set over simmering water, and heat until the chocolate has almost completely melted.

Stir the sugar into the chocolate and lightly whisk in one egg at a time.

Add cardamom, tamarind and hazelnut, mix well, then gently fold in the flour.

Evenly pour the batter into the greased pan and bake until a toothpick inserted in the centre of the cake comes out clean, about 40 to 45 minutes.

Remove the cake from the oven and let it rest for 10 minutes in the pan.

Drizzle with the reserved chocolate sauce and serve warm.

Turmeric

Turmeric

Turmeric (*Curcuma longa*) is a southern Indian native, the plant thrives in shade and fertile alluvial soil, and needs a substantial amount of rainfall, therefore growing well in the monsoon forests of Southeast Asia. India is a major producer of turmeric and a major consumer too.

Belonging to the ginger family, the plant parts include an underground stem and the rhizome, which has roots in the soil and leaves above ground. The roots are hard with a distinct orange-yellow colour. Its white- yellow flowers are hermaphrodite, sterile and do not produce seeds that can germinate.

Turmeric is planted in warm soil in September or October and harvested within 9 to 10 months, when the leaves turn yellow or the stems begin to dry out.

The rhizomes and the tubers are the commonly used parts. The rhizome can be used fresh or dried—it is boiled for up to 45 minutes, and then dried in the sun or the oven before being ground.

Turmeric is used extensively in cooking, as a colouring agent or dye and is also valued for its medicinal properties.

It finds mention in Ayurvedic texts for treating a variety of disorders. In Indian culture, turmeric is considered auspicious and is present in religious ceremonies, weddings and other rituals. Monks use turmeric to dye their robes. The vibrant colour associates it with the sun, which is the energy centre of the universe. In medieval Europe, turmeric was an alternative to saffron and was known as Indian saffron.

Its health benefits are widely known. It contains curcumin, and has anti-inflammatory and detoxification properties. It can also reduce the severity of several disorders.

In culinary terms, turmeric is used in combination with other spices in curry powders, pastes and spice masalas. It imparts a warm flavour and yellow hue to the dishes it is used in, mostly savoury. In the West, it is a colouring agent for mustards and cheese preparations, canned beverages, cakes, etc.

Fresh turmeric finds its way in south Asian recipes as a paste in conjunction with other ingredients such as lemongrass, galangal, garlic, shallots and tamarind; at times, the fresh juice from crushed turmeric is used for rice dishes. In Thailand, the shoots are valued as a vegetable. The fragrant leaves are used in Malaysian cuisine as well as south Indian foods, for wrapping the foods being cooked, to add aroma and a distinct flavour.

Light Fisherman's Soup

Pan Seared Chicken and Zucchini Salad

Baked Mushroom and Chickpea Pouches

Turmeric and Green Papaya Lamb Strips

Marigold and Kiwi Pilaf

Fresh Turmeric, Cashew and
Orange Chutney

Lemongrass and Turmeric Iced Tea

Turmeric and White Chocolate Panna Cotta

Light Fisherman's Soup

This impressive seafood soup is infused with fresh turmeric, ginger and garlic. As the broth cooks, the flavours intermingle, imparting an enhanced taste to the seafood. You can use turmeric powder in place of fresh turmeric.

Serves 4

Ingredients

2 tablespoons olive oil

3 to 4 cloves garlic

2-inch piece of fresh turmeric, peeled and minced

1-inch piece of ginger, minced

3½ cups fish stock

Salt to taste

2 to 3 baby crabs

10 to 12 medium shrimp

6 to 8 ounces halibut

2 medium sized tomatoes, chopped

Juice of 1 lemon

Fresh dill for garnish

Directions

Heat oil in a medium pot over medium heat. Add garlic, turmeric and ginger and sauté for a minute. Pour in the fish stock and salt bring to a boil on high heat.

Add the seafood, reduce the heat to low and simmer, covered, until the seafood is cooked, about 8 to 10 minutes. Occasionally skim off the scum that forms on the surface of the soup. Toss in the tomatoes and mix.

Remove from heat and mix in lemon juice. Garnish with dill and serve hot.

Pan Seared Chicken and Zucchini Salad

Always a welcome addition to any meal, the versatility of chicken salad makes it an all-time favourite. The warm scent and golden colour of turmeric make this salad a must-try. Adding a teaspoon of honey and soy sauce helps create another version.

Serves 4 to 6

Ingredients

3 tablespoons vegetable oil

1 teaspoon turmeric

1-inch piece of ginger, minced

1-inch piece of galangal, minced

2 to 3 kaffir lime leaves

Juice of 1 lemon, divided

Salt to taste

3 (8 ounces each) boneless, skinless chicken breasts, cut into thin strips

1 medium zucchini, sliced

½ cup vegetable or chicken stock, if required

1 bunch mixed greens of your choice

2 tablespoons extra virgin olive oil

½ cup fresh pomegranate seeds

Directions

In a mixing bowl, combine oil, turmeric, ginger, galangal, kaffir lime leaves, half lemon juice and salt. Add chicken and zucchini and toss to coat well. Let it marinate in the refrigerator for at least 30 minutes.

Heat a pan over medium heat and sear the chicken and zucchini for 3 to 4 minutes on each side or until the chicken is cooked through. Add a little vegetable or chicken stock if required to prevent it from burning. Remove from heat and keep warm.

In a medium mixing bowl, toss the greens and pomegranate seeds with olive oil, salt and the remaining lemon juice.

Arrange on a serving platter and top with warm chicken and zucchini to serve.

Baked Mushroom and Chickpea Pouches

These crispy small bites are a party favourite, but it is the versatility of this filling that makes it special. Make sure the filling is not too wet.

Serves 4 to 6

Ingredients

2 tablespoons vegetable oil

4 shallots

1 teaspoon cumin powder

1 pound white mushrooms, finely chopped

1 teaspoon turmeric

1-inch piece of ginger, minced

¼ cup boiled chickpeas, mashed

Salt to taste

½ teaspoon cayenne pepper, or to taste

2 tablespoons cream cheese

½ cup finely chopped spinach leaves

5 sheets phyllo frozen dough, thawed

Melted butter for brushing

24 chives

Directions

In a medium saucepan, heat oil over medium heat. Add shallots and cumin, cook until the shallots are translucent, about 3 minutes, then add mushrooms, turmeric, ginger and chickpeas. Continue to cook until the mixture is dry, 5 to 7 minutes. Remove from heat and add salt, cayenne pepper, cream cheese and spinach leaves and mix well.

On a work surface, place a phyllo sheet and evenly brush it with melted butter. Repeat the process to make a five-layer stack.

With the tip of a sharp knife, cut the sheets into 4-inch squares or a desired shape and size.

Place a generous teaspoon of the mushroom mixture in the centre of a square. Bring the diagonal edges together to create a pouch. Apply a little water to moisten and seal, if required. Repeat with all the phyllo squares.

Place on a baking sheet lined with Silpat and bake for 15 to 20 minutes, until the pouches are golden brown around the edges.

Remove from the oven and tie each pouch with chives. Serve warm with salad and dip of your choice.

Turmeric and Green Papaya Lamb Strips

A quick and easy way to cook a leg of lamb, this dish can be served with a sauce or a dip over salad. Turmeric juice lends its golden glow to the lamb strips as they marinate in a mixture that also has green papaya, garlic and ginger. Stir-frying the lamb keeps it tender inside, while the outside gets browned well.

Serves 4 to 6

Ingredients

4 ounces green papaya, coarsely chopped

1-inch fresh turmeric, peeled

1-inch piece of fresh ginger, peeled

2 cloves garlic

Salt to taste

Juice of 1 lemon

4 tablespoons olive oil

1 pound boneless leg of lamb,
thinly sliced into strips

½ cup radish microgreens

1 teaspoon cayenne pepper (optional)

Directions

In a food processor, pulse green papaya, turmeric, ginger, garlic, salt and lemon juice to a smooth mixture. Add a little olive oil if required.

Transfer the mixture to a mixing bowl, add lamb strips and coat well. Let it marinate in the refrigerator for at least 3 hours.

Heat oil in a large skillet, preferably cast-iron, over medium-high heat. Working in batches, stir-fry the lamb until cooked and golden brown, about 5 to 7 minutes.

Arrange the lamb over radish microgreens, sprinkle with cayenne pepper and serve.

Marigold and Kiwi Pilaf

In Indian culture, marigold is an auspicious flower that graces celebratory events. This flavourful rice pilaf with kiwi is a festive-spirited recipe. With marigold petals tossed in, one whiff of its sweet aroma takes us back to happy memories surrounded by family and friends.

Serves 4

Ingredients

2 tablespoons vegetable oil

1 white onion, finely chopped

1 cup long-grain basmati rice, washed, rinsed, soaked in water for 30 minutes and drained

1 bay leaf

1½ teaspoons turmeric

Salt to taste

2 cups vegetable stock

4 kiwis, peeled and coarsely chopped

2 tablespoons marigold petals

Directions

In a saucepan, heat oil over medium heat. Add onion and sauté until translucent, 2 to 3 minutes. Add rice, bay leaf, turmeric, salt and vegetable stock, bring to a boil over high heat and cook until the liquid is absorbed.

Reduce heat to low, cover the rice with a damp cloth and a tight-fitting lid, and cook for about 5 more minutes. Stir in the kiwi and marigold.

Serve hot.

Fresh Turmeric, Cashew and Orange Chutney

A simple recipe to bottle the earthy and spicy flavours of fresh turmeric, the fresh oranges add a citrusy touch to the chutney. The salty, sweet and gingery pungency of turmeric lends a medley of aroma and flavours.

Fresh turmeric also adds intense colour and provides a healthy kick with its peppier flavour. It's also extremely fragrant.

Makes about 1 cup

Ingredients

3-inch fresh turmeric, peeled

Juice of 1 orange

¼ cup cashews, lightly roasted

1 teaspoon salt, or to taste

½ teaspoon honey

½ teaspoon cayenne pepper, or to taste

Juice of 1 lemon

1 tablespoon extra-virgin olive oil

2 tablespoons finely chopped parsley

Directions

In a food processor, pulse the turmeric, orange juice, cashews, salt, honey, cayenne pepper, lemon juice and oil to a coarse mixture or desired consistency.

Stir in parsley and serve.

Lemongrass and Turmeric Iced Tea

Simmer turmeric root with tea and your daily cuppa will be transformed into a healing and immunity-boosting drink. This iced tea recipe with lemongrass and lemon juice is even more refreshing and shines as a beautiful orange drink.

Serves 4

Ingredients

½ cup sugar

2-inch piece of fresh turmeric, cut into small pieces

2 lemongrass stalks

1 star anise

Juice of 1 lemon, or as required

4 green tea bags

Pinch of salt

Directions

In a small saucepan, combine all the ingredients together over medium heat until the sugar dissolves. Remove from heat and let the flavours steep while cooling to room temperature. Remove the tea bags.

To serve, pour the drink over ice and top with chilled water, seltzer or champagne.

Turmeric and White Chocolate Panna Cotta

The creamy dessert gets a new avatar with turmeric. A rather unusual addition to a panna cotta, turmeric adds a warm, spicy flavour and deep rich colour. Topped with passion fruit syrup, this recipe is as visually stunning as it is delicious.

Serves 4 to 6

Ingredients

1 envelope (¼ ounce) unflavoured gelatin

1 cup heavy cream

1 cup whole milk

¼ cup sugar or to taste, plus 1 teaspoon

Pinch of salt

½ teaspoon turmeric

3 passion fruit pulp

Pinch of ground cardamom

Directions

In ¼ cup cold water, sprinkle in gelatin and whisk to dissolve. Set aside to bloom or soften for 5 to 10 minutes.

In a medium saucepan, cook cream, milk, sugar, salt and turmeric over medium heat until the sugar dissolves. Remove from heat, add gelatin and stir until well dissolved.

Divide the mixture into small containers or moulds of your choice. Chill in the refrigerator for 4 hours, preferably overnight.

In a saucepan over medium heat, cook the passion fruit pulp with 2 tablespoons of water, 1 teaspoon of sugar and cardamom powder until the sugar dissolves. Remove from heat and chill.

Top chilled panna cotta with the passion fruit mix and serve.

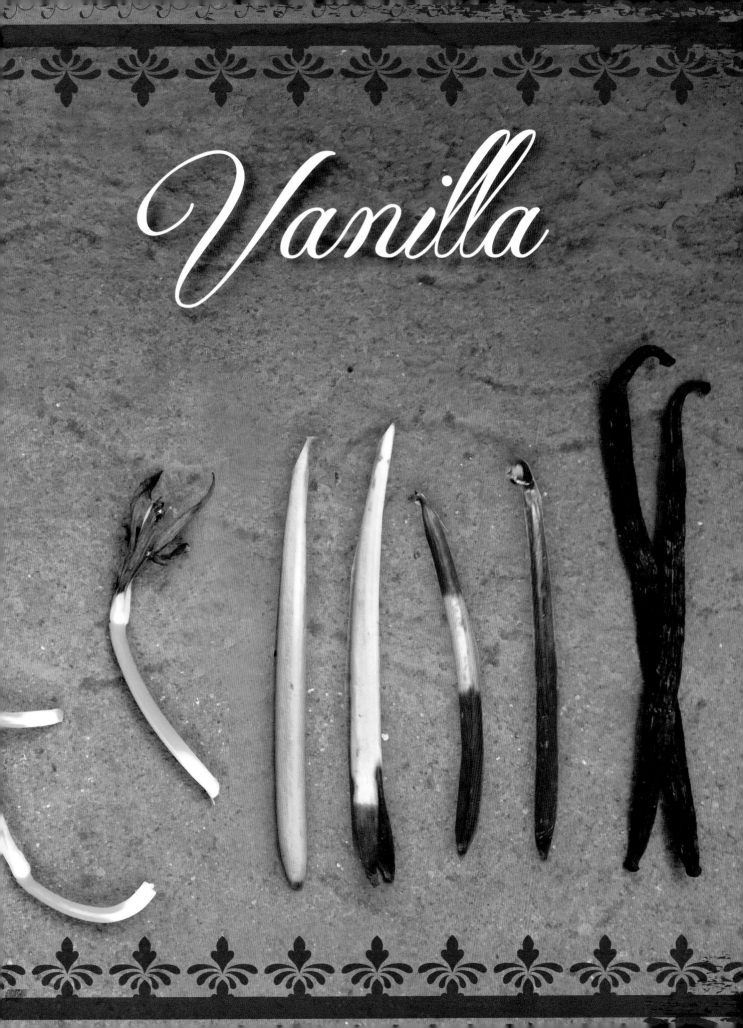

Vanilla

Vanilla

The orchids of the genus vanilla, mainly from the Mexican species *Vanilla planifolia*, bear the fruit from which vanilla flavouring is derived. The word vanilla has its origins in the Spanish word vaina, which means little pod. The Spanish introduced vanilla to Europe.

Vanilla was originally cultivated in what is Veracruz today in Mexico. When the Aztecs conquered the area then known as Totonacs, they named the fruit they began to develop a taste for—*tlilxochitl* or black flower—as it matures and takes a black shrivelled form after being picked.

Since the local Melipona bee in Central America was the natural pollinator for the vanilla orchid, early efforts to grow vanilla in other regions were not successful. However, later discoveries made this possible when it was realised that pollination could be done by hand.

At present three types of vanilla are grown around the world—vanilla planifolia around the Indian Ocean such as in Madagascar, Indonesia and Réunion; vanilla tahitensis in the South Pacific; and vanilla pompona, found in the West Indies, Central and South America, all originating from the original genus from present-day Mexico. The major variety is the first one, another name for which is creamy Bourbon vanilla. Madagascar and Indonesia produce majority of the vanilla in the global scenario.

The cultivation of vanilla is labour-intensive. Vanilla is prized for its flavour, obtained from the fruit compounds that are a result of pollination. Each flower produces one brown-red vanilla pod, that changes to black when ripe. It is filled with tiny seeds and a liquid of oily consistency. The flowers contain both the anther and stigma, and are pollinated by the mountain bee or by hand. For years this created a problem of growing vanilla outside Mexico, as it would grow but not flower. The bees transfer pollen by getting under a flap inside the flower; this process was eventually imitated by hand. Using a bamboo sliver, grass stem or wood splinter, the worker lifts the membrane between the male and female organs of the flower and press anther into the stigma, thus transferring the pollen resulting in the production of the fruit. As the flower is in bloom only for one day or less, the cultivators have to check for open flowers daily. Pollination must occur within 12 hours of the opening of the flower; only one flower opens per day.

The fruit develops in about six weeks and takes six months to ripen.

The best time for planting in tropical areas is September to November; flowering occurs in the spring.

As the pods mature, the dark green fruit develops a yellow discolouration at the fruit's end. The fruit needs to be picked just as it begins to split from the end to ensure the best flavour. The market value of each pod is based on how it looks and its length; 6 inches and more is an indicator of best quality reserved for the gourmet market.

The fruit containing thousands of black seeds needs to be cured to get better value. This process is responsible for the aroma - heating, freezing or scratching the fruit along the length, or by heating in the oven or drying in direct sunlight, which was the traditional method used by the Aztecs. Different methods produce different profiles.

At the end of the process, the fruits acquire their brown colour and most of the flavour and aroma.

The fruit is then conditioned for about six months by storing in closed boxes to develop the fragrance. They are then finally sorted and graded. They are graded based on length, colour, sheen, and moisture content, the best quality being, dark, plump, oily whole pods with no blemishes. These are prized in gourmet cooking, while lower quality vanilla is used to extract flavouring. However, the highest grade is not necessarily the most flavourful as it might not contain the most vanillin.

The second-most expensive spice after saffron, vanilla's extract is used extensively in food, aromatherapy and perfumes. Vanilla grown in different regions has its own distinct notes. Madagascar has the Bourbon variety, which is rich and creamy; the Mexican variety is delicate and complex, the Tahitian floral or fruity, while Indonesian is strong and smoky. Givre is the French term for the white frosting that appears on the beans due to vanillin crystals.

The beans are used whole or by splitting in desserts like ice creams, custards, etc., with tiny seeds indicating the presence of vanilla in the preparation. The whole bean can be rinsed, dried and used again. French vanilla is a preparation with a strong aroma of vanilla usually mixed with egg and contains tiny grains. It may also contain other flavourings such as caramel and butterscotch. Vanilla pairs extremely well with chocolate but it also works well as a spice with savoury recipes that has ingredients such as root vegetables, seafood, chicken and fruits.

Stored in an airtight container, the pods can last up to two years.

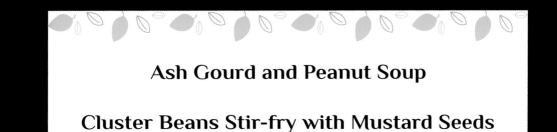

Ash Gourd and Peanut Soup

Cluster Beans Stir-fry with Mustard Seeds

Braised Chicken Legs with Semolina Porridge

Garlicky Butter Beans with Cilantro

Spiced Bulgur with Poached Pears

Sweet Mango Risotto

Pineapple-Mango Medley with Figs

Orange Cardamom Cake

Ash Gourd and Peanut Soup

This ash gourd soup retains all the healthy properties of the fruit. Its mild fresh taste is a good base, great for stews, curries and juices. Ash gourd adapts well with other ingredients; here, vanilla enrich the taste of this nutritious soup.

Serves 4

Ingredients

2 tablespoons peanuts

1 teaspoon coriander seeds

2 dried red chillies

2 tablespoons peanut oil

2 cloves garlic, minced

1 medium red onion, finely chopped

2 cups ash gourd, peeled, seeded and cut into cubes

Salt to taste

½ vanilla bean, split

3 cups vegetable stock

½ cup heavy cream

Microgreens for garnish

Directions

In a small skillet, dry-roast peanuts, coriander and chillies until fragrant, stirring continuously. Remove from heat and grind to a coarse mixture in a coffee or spice grinder.

Heat the oil in a medium pan. Add garlic and onion and sauté until the latter is translucent, about 3 minutes. Add the ash gourd, salt, vanilla bean, stock and heavy cream and bring to a boil over high heat. Then, reduce the heat to low, and simmer, covered, for about 20 minutes, until the mixture is creamy and fragrant. Remove the vanilla bean.

Transfer the soup to a blender and process until smooth. Add a little water if required for desired consistency.

Garnish with the peanut mixture and microgreens.

Serve hot.

Cluster Beans Stir-fry with Mustard Seeds

Native to India, cluster beans are a tasty legume similar to green beans. Many stir-fries in South Indian cooking are quick, easy and versatile, and the ingredients are easy to substitute. For me, it is the addition of coconut that brings the region's authentic flavour and texture to these dishes.

You can use green beans or any other vegetable in this recipe instead of cluster beans.

Serves 4 to 6

Ingredients

2 tablespoons coconut oil

1 medium red onion, finely chopped

1 teaspoon mustard seeds

½ vanilla bean, split

30 to 40 cluster beans, washed, dried and split lengthwise

1 teaspoon turmeric

1 teaspoon garlic powder

½ dried ginger powder

Salt to taste

Freshly ground black pepper

½ cup grated coconut

Directions

Heat oil in a saucepan over medium heat. Add onion, mustard seeds and vanilla and sauté until fragrant and the onion is translucent, about 3 to 4 minutes. Add the cluster beans, season with turmeric, garlic and ginger powders, salt and pepper and mix well.

Reduce the heat to low, cover and cook until the flavours merge and the beans are cooked. Remove the vanilla and mix in the coconut. Serve hot.

Braised Chicken Legs with Semolina Porridge

Braising is a great technique for cooking chicken legs and thighs. The chicken is first pan seared over high heat then cooked in a low simmer until it's tender. Additional ingredients and flavourings help make this recipe a complete meal in itself.

Serves 4

Ingredients

4 (about 12 ounces each) whole chicken legs

Salt to taste

Freshly ground black pepper

2 teaspoons chipotle paste

2 tablespoons tamarind paste

2 cloves garlic, minced

6 tablespoons vegetable or canola oil

½ vanilla bean, scraped

Juice of 1 lemon

1 medium red onion, finely chopped

2 medium tomatoes, chopped

1 teaspoon cumin powder

1 teaspoon cayenne pepper, or to taste

2 tablespoons tomato puree

1 cup vegetable stock

2 carrots, cut into batons, steamed and lightly salted

Mint leaves for garnish

For semolina porridge

1 tablespoon vegetable or canola oil

½ cup semolina

1 teaspoon curry powder

Salt to taste

Juice of 1 lemon

Directions

In a mixing bowl, add chicken legs, salt, pepper, chipotle, tamarind, garlic, 2 tablespoons of oil, vanilla and lemon juice. Toss to coat well and let it marinate in the refrigerator for at least 3 hours.

In a saucepan, heat 2 tablespoons of oil over medium heat. Sauté the onion until translucent, about 3 minutes, then add tomatoes, cumin, salt and cayenne pepper. Cook until the tomatoes begin to dry, stirring continuously. Add tomato puree and stock and bring to a boil. Remove from heat and keep warm.

In a large cast-iron or heavy-bottom skillet, heat 2 tablespoons of oil over high heat. Sear the chicken until golden brown, about 3 to 4 minutes each side, turning gently. Add the tomato mixture and cook on low heat, covered, until the chicken is cooked through and the flavours merge.

Remove from heat and keep warm.

To make the semolina porridge, heat the oil in a saucepan over medium-low heat. Add the semolina and stir continuously for 2 to 3 minutes until fragrant, then add curry powder, salt and 1 cup water (or as required) for desired consistency. Cover and cook for 3 minutes until the mixture comes together.

Stir in the lemon juice and serve with chicken and carrots, garnished with mint leaves.

Garlicky Butter Beans with Cilantro

Even though these beans take a long time to cook, it is worth the time and effort. Taste the delicate and mild beans with a starchy texture, which gives a hearty character to this recipe.

Serves 4 to 6

Ingredients

2 tablespoons unsalted butter

1 medium white onion, finely chopped

2 cloves garlic, minced

½ cup butter beans, rinsed, soaked overnight and drained

½ vanilla bean, split

3½ to 4 cups vegetable stock, or as required

Salt to taste

1 tomato, seeded and chopped

2 tablespoons freshly chopped cilantro

Directions

Heat butter in a saucepan over medium heat. Add onion and garlic and sauté until the onion turns translucent, about 3 minutes. Add the butter beans and vanilla and stir well.

Pour in the vegetable stock and salt and bring to a boil. Reduce the heat to low, cover and cook until the butter beans are tender, about 1 hour and 45 minutes to 2 hours. Stir in the tomato.

Remove the vanilla, garnish with cilantro and serve hot.

Spiced Bulgur with Poached Pears

In this recipe, an interesting combination of ingredients comes together—spiced bulgur with sweet, smooth pears poached in vanilla-flavoured white wine.

Serves 4

Ingredients

2 tablespoons vegetable oil

1 star anise

1-inch cinnamon stick

1 cup cracked bulgur

1½ cups vegetable stock

1 teaspoon vanilla extract, divided

Salt to taste

1 cup dry white wine

2 Bartlett or Bosc pears

1 vanilla bean, scraped

1 cup fresh rucola leaves

Directions

Heat oil in a large skillet over medium heat. Add star anise, cinnamon and bulgur and cook, stirring frequently, until golden and fragrant, about 4 to 5 minutes. Pour in the stock, ½ teaspoon of vanilla extract and salt and bring to a boil over medium-high heat.

Reduce heat to low, cover and cook until the bulgur is tender, and the liquid has been absorbed, about 10 minutes. Remove the cinnamon and keep warm.

In a saucepan, combine white wine, the remaining vanilla extract and a pinch of salt and gently poach the pears for 3 to 4 minutes. Cool to room temperature.

Cut the pears into strips. Serve with bulgur and rucola leaves.

Sweet Mango Risotto

A vanilla twist to silky risotto with diced yellow mangoes uplift this dish both in appearance and taste. I love finishing it off with coconut milk for a nice aftertaste and fragrance. Arborio rice is perfect for creamy risotto while retaining its shape.

Serves 4 to 6

Ingredients

4 cups whole milk

½ cup honey

2½ teaspoons vanilla extract

2 tablespoons clarified butter

1 cup Arborio rice

1-inch piece of ginger, finely chopped

1 teaspoon orange zest

¼ cup coconut milk

2 ripe mangoes, peeled, pitted and diced

Fresh mint leaves for garnish

Directions

In a medium pan, heat milk, honey and vanilla over medium heat until bubbles form around the edges. Reduce the heat to low, cover and cook for 2 to 3 minutes. Remove and keep warm.

Melt butter in a medium saucepan over medium heat. Add the rice and stir for about 2 to 3 minutes, then add ginger and orange zest and continue to cook. Gradually add the milk mixture while stirring vigorously, and cook until the milk mixture is absorbed and the mixture is thick like porridge, about 20 to 25 minutes.

Add coconut milk and mangoes and give it a stir. Garnish with mint leaves and serve.

Pineapple-Mango Medley with Figs

Sweet pineapple and mango juice with tart lime strike a balance of flavours that are sweet, citrusy and not too sour. Ripe figs are a great addition to cocktails such as in this recipe.

Serves 4

Ingredients

1 cup pineapple juice

1 vanilla bean, scraped and split lengthwise into 4 strips

Juice of 1 lime

1 cup mango juice

1 teaspoon pink salt

2 to 3 figs, coarsely chopped, for garnish

Directions

In a pitcher, mix the pineapple juice, vanilla, lime juice, mango juice and pink salt.

To serve, pour over ice and garnish with chopped figs and vanilla strips.

Orange Cardamom Cake

This sweet bread-like dessert is synonymous with celebration. There are countless cake recipes available and many more flavour combinations waiting to be discovered. But no matter the recipe, cakes with fruit, preserves, nuts, icing, frosting or sprinkles are seldom turned down.

Serves 4 to 6

Ingredients

For the orange sauce

1 cup orange juice

2 teaspoons corn starch

1 tablespoon honey

1 teaspoon orange zest

1 teaspoon lemon juice

For cake

Cooking spray for greasing

2 cups all-purpose flour, plus more for dusting

1 cup sugar

1 vanilla bean, scraped

1 cup unsalted butter

4 eggs

1 teaspoon cardamom powder

1 teaspoon baking powder

Directions

Preheat the oven to 350°F.

To make orange sauce, whisk the orange juice and corn starch in a mixing bowl into a smooth mixture. Transfer to a pan and cook on medium heat, whisking continuously. Add honey, orange zest and lemon juice and continue to cook until the mixture is thick, whisking continuously. Remove from heat and cool at room temperature.

Grease an 8½ × 4½-inch loaf pan, lightly dust with flour and set aside.

In a medium mixing bowl, whisk sugar, vanilla and butter with an electric eggbeater until light and fluffy. Add one egg at a time, beating continuously. Reduce the speed to low and gradually add cardamom, flour and baking soda and mix well. It is very important for this batter to be light.

Pour the batter into the greased pan. Swirl in 4 tablespoons of the orange sauce. Bake until a toothpick inserted in the centre of the cake comes out clean, about 45 minutes to 1 hour. Remove the cake from the oven and cool in the baking pan for about 15 minutes.

Serve warm or at room temperature with the orange sauce.

Index

Ceremony of Aromas | INDEX

French Mustard Cake 243
Fresh Turmeric, Cashew and Orange Chutney 349
Frittata 215
Fruit 8, 14, 59, 72, 92, 107, 112, 130, 150, 170, 175, 195,
 203, 208, 215, 223, 235, 243, 246, 247, 253, 273, 275,
 291, 298, 301, 318, 333, 353, 356, 357, 359, 373
  candied 333
  chopped 275
  citrus 291
  poaching 298
  star-shaped 298
  tropical 246
Frying 51, 115, 121, 153, 213, 219, 327, 345
  shallow- 121
Fuyu persimmons 69

Gailon broccoli 191
Galangal 75, 137, 150, 336, 341
  soup 75
Garam masala 92, 123, 130, 247, 298
Garam masala mix 92
Garlic 19, 23, 25, 37, 41, 43, 59, 63, 75, 79, 81, 92, 95, 101,
 103, 115, 117, 121, 123, 125, 137, 139, 141, 143, 150,
 153, 155, 159, 175, 177, 179, 191, 193, 195, 197, 199,
 211, 213, 229, 237, 239, 249, 253, 255, 263, 265, 267,
 271, 281, 283, 285, 301, 303, 307, 321, 323, 325, 327,
 329, 336, 339, 345, 359, 361, 363, 365
  chives 307
  powder 95, 115, 199, 325, 361
Garlicky Butter Beans with Cilantro 365
Garnishing 19, 21, 23, 27, 29, 31, 37, 45, 59, 61, 65, 67, 77,
 79, 81, 83, 85, 87, 89, 92, 99, 101, 105, 107, 115, 119,
 133, 139, 143, 145, 153, 155, 157, 159, 161, 163, 165,
 173, 175, 185, 191, 195, 197, 205, 221, 226, 227, 229,
 237, 239, 251, 253, 255, 267, 269, 271, 273, 275, 281,
 285, 287, 305, 307, 313, 315, 321, 325, 327, 329, 339,
 359, 363, 365, 369, 371
Gelatin 353
Ginger 21, 25, 34, 49, 59, 75, 77, 81, 99, 117, 123, 125, 135,
 145, 150, 153, 155, 157, 159, 161, 163, 165, 167, 173,
 179, 185, 197, 203, 205, 213, 229, 237, 251, 269, 283,
 291, 295, 301, 303, 305, 313, 325, 329, 336, 339, 341,
 343, 345, 361, 369
  ale 150
  baby 150
  beer 150
  bleached 150
  candied 150, 161, 167
  chopped 165
  crystallised 150
  dried powder 135, 167, 203, 361
  dry 150

  green 150
  ground 150
  juice 21, 49, 145, 157, 185, 205, 213, 283
  leaves 150
  nature 150
  pickled 251
  unbleached 150
  wild flower 150
  young 150
Ginger Chicken Soup 153
Ginger-garlic paste 150
Ginger Saffron Yogurt Cake 295
Ginger-Scented Creamy Mustard Greens 237
Ginger-Star Anise Apple Juice 313
Gooseberries 67, 89
Gouda 287
Grapefruit Ginger Medley 49
Grapeseed 43, 213
  oil 43, 213
Gravy 247, 327
  tomato 327
  Tomato-Rhubarb 327
Green Chartreuse 145
Green Mango and Lamb Salad 175
Green Mango Pilaf 271
Green Papaya Lamb Strips 345
Green Peas Creamy Risotto 47
Green Peppercorns and Honey Prawns 23
Grilled Chicken in Smoky Mustard Oil 233
Grilling 45
Guacamole 41

Habanero 201
  orange 201
Halibut 139
Handcrafted Orange Zest Olives 135
Harissa 92
Hazelnut 29, 69, 137, 333
  roasted 29, 69
Hazelnut Basil Dressing Salad 137
Hearty Onion Soup with Fennel 133
Herb 92, 130, 188, 226, 227, 298
  culinary 188
  stuffing 227
  warming 298
Herbalism 72
Herring 235
  boneless 235
Homemade Gingerade 165
Honey 23, 29, 49, 63, 87, 89, 137, 150, 199, 201, 213, 231,
 265, 291, 341, 349, 369, 373
  Prawns 23

About the Author

VIKAS KHANNA is an internationally acclaimed Indian American chef, film-maker and author. He is a James Beard nominee and one of the first Indian chefs to be awarded a Michelin Star for his restaurant in the US.

He has been featured among the ten most influential chefs in the world by Deutsche Welle and Gazette Review. He is the host of *MasterChef India, Twist of Taste* and *India's Megakitchens* on National Geographic. Khanna is the author of 38 books, including *Utsav: A Culinary Epic of Indian Festivals* (world's most expensive cookbook) and the creator of the documentary series *Holy Kitchens* and *Kitchens of Gratitude*.

He founded the Museum of Kitchen Arts, which is home to thousands of India's unique kitchen tools and equipment, at his alma mater, WGSHA, Manipal, India.

His restaurants, Kinara and Ellora, are rated as Dubai's favourite Indian restaurants by *Condé Nast*.

His initiative Feed India served more than 51 million meals during the Covid-19 pandemic. *The Last Color*, which was considered for the best feature film award at the 2020 Academy Awards, marked Khanna's debut as a film writer and director.